The Collector's Garden

The Collector's Garden

Designing with Extraordinary Plants

KEN DRUSE

Edited by Margaret Roach
Design by Richard Ferretti

TIMBER PRESS
Portland • Cambridge

FOR MARCIA, MARCO, MARGARET, MARY, AND MOM
and to Jim Cross, who was an inspiration to all who knew him

Published in 2004 by

Timber Press, Inc.
The Haseltine Building
133 S.W. Second Avenue, Suite 450
Portland, Oregon 97204-3527, U.S.A.
www.timberpress.com

Timber Press
2 Station Road
Swavesey
Cambridge CB4 5QJ, U.K.

Printed in Hong Kong

Library of Congress Cataloging-in-Publication Data
Druse, Kenneth.
    The collector's garden : designing wih extraordinary plants / Ken Druse ;
edited by Margaret Roach ; design by Richard Ferretti
        p. cm.
    Originally published: New York : Clarkson Potter, c1996.
    Includes bibliographical references and index.
    ISBN 0-88192-660-4 (pbk.)
    I. Gardens. 2. Plant collectors—Homes and haunts. 3. Plant introduction.
    4. Plants, Ornamental. I. Roach, Margaret. II. Title.
SB454.D78 2004
580'.75—dc22

                                                        2004049815

A catalog record for this book is also available from the British Library.

FRONTISPIECE: *The Bellevue Botanical Garden border (pages 175–76)*.
OPPOSITE: Digitalis purpurea *and* Geranium × *'Johnson's Blue'*.
ABOVE: Caltha palustris *flower in Jerry Flintoff's garden (pages 187–90)*.
FOLLOWING PAGES, LEFT TO RIGHT: *Harold Epstein's thirty-year-old* Enkianthus perulatus *'Nana' (pages 29–31)*. Papaver nudicale; Tovara virginiana *'Variegata'*.
PREFACE: Arisaema candidissima.

ACKNOWLEDGMENTS

I met the most wonderful people researching this book and traveling across the country. Frankly, I was surprised to find so many "plant nuts," as some of these people call themselves. In addition to all those in this book, I would like to extend special thanks to friends and supporters: Alberto Vitale, Anne Lovejoy, Barbara Marks, Bobbi and Michael Fischer, Diane Frieden, Dick Turner, Eliza Reed, Franklin Salasky, Gail Shanks, Gary Peese, Helen and Harold Druse, Helen Pratt, Howard Klein, Isolde Motley, James Blaze, James deGrey David, Jane Treuhaft, Joanna and Peter Bristol, Jody Lathwell, Joe Querolo, Jo Fagan, John Emanuel, John Nally, Jose Concepcion, Julia Morris, Kate French, Kathy Ann Miller, Kevin Bost, Kris Jarantoski, Lauren Shakely, Laurie Stark, Leah Carlson, Louis Bauer, Marcia Donahue, Marco Polo Stufano, Margaret Roach, Mark McCauslin, Martha Stewart, Michelle Sidrane, Nancy Maloney, Patrick Smith, Richard Ferretti, Robin Parer, Robin Strashun, Sonny Garcia, Stan Farwig, Teresa Nicholas, and Tina Constable.

CONTENTS

PREFACE

I never met a plant I didn't like. Seeing a new one and then collecting it for my garden is my magnificent obsession. I may happen upon an unfamiliar plant while traveling. To the locals, it's nothing special. To me, it's a wonder, and I wonder whether I can find one of my own and grow it. On other occasions, gardeners may usher me through their landscape to a place of honor where lies their most precious jewel: the latest, greatest entry in the world of horticulture. If I believe I can grow it and can barter or beg a piece, I'll bag it. The search begins and nearly always ends when the acquisition makes itself at home in my garden.

This book grew out of my last one, *The Natural Habitat Garden,* which is about gardening with native plants. In that work, my coauthor Margaret Roach and I suggested planting portions of landscapes large and small with the kinds of botanical communities that might have grown on the site in the years before development. I recommended that other plantings (of exotics) be thought of as collections, corralled or contained, the way that beds and borders, foundation plantings, and even lawns are.

My own 20-by-50-foot plot in Brooklyn, New York, contains plenty of great natives, but more than anything else, it is a collector's garden. It is contained by buildings, concrete, and asphalt—the perfect place for well-behaved exotic plants and indigenous ones, as well. I've also designed a habitat-style city park in my neighborhood with indigenous plants similar to the ones that grew in this habitat before New York was a city.

Although I believe in conserving our native plants and preserving wild areas, I can't give up some of my favorites from abroad. It is most important that these plants know their place—that is, that they are not invasive. Hostas, for example, originated halfway round the world, but are at home in my shady garden. They increase slowly, barely at all; there is no danger of a *Hosta* takeover.

As I began to research and photograph this book, I was thrilled to find so many plant nuts like me. Members of one group in Northern California call themselves the Hortisexuals. Their motto: "No plant is safe." If they see it and like it, they've got to have it. A few members of this serious but light-hearted group are featured in this book. As obsessed as they may be, the Hortisexuals and other collectors tend to have gardens that are modest, doable creations—not million-dollar installations or grand estates. For space considerations, I could not profile the growers of thousands of hostas or daylilies and had to forgo collectors of greenhouse tropicals and growers of exotic and heritage food crops. What they all have in common is their tremendous passion and a hands-on approach.

When I wrote to one collector, Jim Waddick of Kansas City, Missouri, asking to visit him, he responded that he had no garden. In a sense, he was right, yet my trip there was inspirational. Although he didn't have conventional beds with tidy paths and orderly borders, he had scores of plants in pots, and others were plopped in spaces where they would do the best, even in the cracks in the pavement. They weren't weeds to him, either; they took precedence and had to be stepped over. He wasn't about to pull out or trample a precious specimen just when he discovered the ideal circumstances for success.

My idea of a garden is liberal enough to welcome many definitions, many styles, so long as the plant selection is daring. In *The Collector's Garden,* the plants star.

Often, the unusual features of some plants attract collectors more than the obvious beauty of, say, a rose flower. The pleated leaves of Uvularia per-foliata, OPPOSITE, *look as if they have been sewn together with a zigzag stitch. Unconventional elegance is evident in the winter-blooming* Helleborus orientalis *flowers,* LEFT, *and color comes from the striped foliage of* Canna 'Pretoria', ABOVE.

Introduction

If it's rare, we want it. If it's tiny and impossible to grow, we've got to have it. If it's brown, looks dead, and has black flowers, we'll kill for it.

We're collectors and little will stand in the way of bagging our quarry. We are driven by a must-have passion that singles us out from other gardeners.

The world of plant collectors is certainly one of the most exciting subcultures in horticulture, a peculiar community within the green scene. If you keep at gardening long enough, sooner or later, you'll become a collector. The plants at the local garden center just won't be enough to feed your appetite or paint the garden picture of your dreams, and the desire to possess the newest botanical curiosity will be stronger than you can stand. At that moment, you unwittingly become a member of the select collector's group.

Collectors come in various guises, and for this book, I have given them names. Some are *hunters*, part of a long tradition of people who have sought out the new and the different. Other collectors are *missionaries*, driven to save threatened plants by growing them in conservancy collections, or to spread the word about their favorites. Many collectors are impressed by a taxonomic group of plants or a particular habitat and become *specialists*. *Aesthetes* collect plants for their appearance and value in garden designs.

Though the psychology probably has much in common with that of other collectors—the antique-car connoisseurs and philatelists more than the tag-sale junkies who bring home anything and everything—there is something more here: commitment. Plants are among the highest-maintenance collectibles. But gardeners have a need to nurture, and in collectors, this need is especially keen, because very often, the more rare and odd their charges, the tougher it is to keep them happy, or even alive. Not surprisingly, many collectors represented here have adult children or none at all—the more energy to put into their botanical charges.

Unlike precious antiques, our obsessions reproduce, so their status as one-of-a-kind rarities may be fleeting. Imagine if an emerald could, with the help of guiding hands, be cloned into an endless number of like progeny. That can be the case with a rare plant. Sometimes the process is arduous, but in most situations, rare plants have the same biological imperative to reproduce as any other living thing.

Some people collect just for the joy of acquisition. The thinking goes, if it looks good and you don't have it, get it. Accumulating is not collecting, although often, we get so wrapped up in the garage-sale mentality that we will purchase nearly anything just in case, someday, we may want it. Marco Polo Stufano of Wave Hill in the Bronx, New York (pages 209–15), has an antidote for such binges. He won't grow any plant he hasn't seen. He needs to know in advance that it will reward his time and effort.

To others, there is a great thrill in being the first on the block, in the neighborhood, state, country, world, to possess a botanical rarity—no matter what it looks like.

The first trophy I bagged was actually more of a rescue. It was a seedling of a *Liriodendron tulipifera*, the tulip tree, a straight-growing native used for telephone poles. I found it lying in the street, having fallen out of a crack in the curbstone where it sprouted. I picked it up and rushed home. My mother helped me plant it on our property in New Jersey. (I was also the kid who rescued the baby birds and abandoned bunnies.)

My early inspiration came from Ernesta and Fred Ballard, whose potted plants and bonsai summer beneath their pergola, ABOVE. When I moved to New York City, I began a roof garden, OPPOSITE, BELOW, collecting plants that could stand blazing sun and temperature extremes, including old-fashioned sunflowers and single hollyhocks. OPPOSITE, ABOVE: Streaked tulips, similar to this modern, virus-free 'Princess Irene', inspired the tulipomania of the seventeenth century.

My earliest interests were the woodland wildflowers. I have had a fascination with *Arisaema triphyllum* since childhood. I was mesmerized by the little hooded spadix, and by the name Jack-in-the-pulpit when my mother told it to me and explained its meaning. I also clearly remember being told to never, ever, pick one (or any wildflower)—another legacy of my mother, who, though not a devout gardener, worships nature. I would never *collect* in the sense of taking plants from the wild, but I have learned ethical ways to find nearly any specimen I desire.

My other passions seem to arise from my circumstances. I was a devotee of houseplants (like everyone else) in the 1970s. I was fascinated by the tropicals I could grow in my tiny apartment, under fluorescent lights in the bathroom. I would start enough seeds every winter to fill a greenhouse, only to end up giving all but one of each away when it became clear that they were going to turn into plants that required windowsill space. My appetite for the unusual became voracious with the encouragement of a single book—*Garden in Your House* by Ernesta Ballard (1971).

When I lived in Providence, Rhode Island, I went to Logee's Greenhouses in nearby Danielson, Connecticut, at a friend's recommendation. Because of the trips to Logee's, where I saw thousands of scented geraniums, citrus plants, aroids, and begonias, my interest catapulted in the direction that changed my life—toward the career I have today.

When I moved to a top-floor, 8,000-square-foot loft in the SoHo neighborhood of New York City, I realized a dream: to have a greenhouse. I built a 20-foot-by-16-foot fiberglass and wood structure on the roof that you entered from the floor below through an old skylight opening above a spiral staircase. Soon I ventured out onto the roof and gardened in containers. My collecting took a turn. I began to seek plants that bloomed despite severe summer's heat and wind up on the roof; plants that could stand winter freezing in containers. What resulted was a garden of prairie plants: *Echinacea, Liatris, Baptisia, Thermopsis, Rudbeckia,* and *Helianthus.*

When I moved to a shaded garden in Brooklyn, New York, I turned back to the woodland plants—back to Jack. As I puttered around trying not to curse the darkness, I found I could bring light in with variegated plants. I had never liked these, but I didn't really know them, either. I was familiar with a handful of cream-edged hostas and speckled ivies, but when I saw how intricate variegation could be, I went wild: painted dogwoods, striped reeds, checked vines. Today, variegation is one of my obsessions.

Since I have lived in cities for most of my gardening life, my plants usually arrive with the post. Favorites come from

Logee's, now three hours away. My gardening year still begins with the arrival of the spring catalogs.

Catalogs have nearly always been a part of horticulture—not just in the hundred-plus years of the Burpee Annual, but throughout the history of Europe and our country. John Bartram's collection in Philadelphia (page 27), the first botanical garden in America, produced a catalog in 1773 listing the plants he grew. Collectors in Europe funded his expeditions to find new and unusual plants for commerce as food or medicinal crops, and also as ornamentals for estates specializing in trees or shrubs, for example, and for nurseries that propagated and sold vast lots of plants for gardeners more than two hundred years ago.

Plant collecting has a rich, if somewhat checkered, history. Perhaps the most extreme case was the mad pursuit of the tulip in the Netherlands in the 1630s. Tulips had first been imported to Europe from Turkey in the 1500s, and by 1573, the botanist Carolus Clusius had some 600 variations in his physic garden in Vienna. A few of these exist today in antique collections.

The first mention of streaked, multicolored flowers was around 1580. The "broken" tulips, made variegated by a virus, were introduced to the Netherlands and created a sensation. Prices rose rapidly to astronomic heights, and in 1637, the third year of the tulip craze, the entire economy and the stock market of the Netherlands was based on these bulbs. Noblemen traded and sold their prized flowers for what today might have been tens of thousands of dollars, but *Tulpenwindhandel,* or tulipomania, swept every class. In addition to their life savings in florins, tulipomaniacs bartered livestock, grain, household goods, cheese, and clothes. Some indulgent parents even gave tulips as dowries. In one tale, a seaman inadvertently ate a bulb thinking it was an onion—a shockingly exorbitant repast. The market became flooded with enthusiasts wanting to sell and a saturated public unwilling to buy. The market crashed, leaving sadder but wiser investors and a nation to this day identified with a single—no longer rare—plant.

Today's new plants tend to follow trends and fads, too. The British garden author and plantswoman Dilys Davies recently remarked that "it's really tony to match everything to dirt—gray, brown, pewter." One proof of this trend is the current fad for the humble *Heuchera* (alum root). With

Some collectors have a wonderful preoccupation with foliage and flowers in dusky colors, especially gray, black, purple, and brown. Chocolate cosmos (Cosmos atrosanguineus), BELOW LEFT, *is not only reddish-brown, but smells like cocoa. Many new* Heucheras, BELOW RIGHT, *with pewter-, bronze-, and copper-colored foliage, are available.*

names like 'Pewter Veil' and 'Chocolate Ruffles', it takes the maturing eye of a collector who has transcended astilbes and marigolds to take the second look, then recognize and covet (or reject) the unconventional. Sophisticated or not, I finally banished the mocha-brown, grasslike plant *Carex buchananii* after the forty-fifth person asked me if it was dead.

Several years ago, the most sought after plant was the brown-and-white-flowered Japanese Jack-in-the-pulpit, *Arisaema sikokianum.* Nearly every gardener I visited would take me aside and whisper, "There's something over here that I'll bet you've never seen the likes of." I didn't have to be polite and pretend to be impressed—I am always exhilarated to see this plant, and the better it's grown and the more perfectly it presents its striking inflorescence, the more taken I am by its exotic beauty. (I can easily predict that the Chinese pink-and-white species, *Arisaema candidissima,* will be the miraculous collectible soon. It already is in my garden.)

It is not just boasting to flaunt your prizes or to advertise your obsession. I have revealed my passion, an infatuation with *Arisaema,* to similarly infatuated gardeners, and they have helped me find sources for these elusive beings. These people also share seeds and tubers. Admire to acquire—as the old saying goes.

Some gardens are large; others are not. Budd Myers tends a Lilliputian world on a chunk of tufa rock, ABOVE. *Literally hundreds of tiny alpine plants live on this mountainside in miniature.*

Arisaema is still unusual, but by no means the oddest of collectibles. In Japan, there is the art of *koten engei*—a system of growing plants in pots, which dates back several hundred years at least, with roots in China and Korea. We know little about this tradition that is more popular there than bonsai. The technique involves growing plant mutations in decorative pots—very often, some of the hundreds of wild ginger (*Asarum*) variations, plants without showy flowers. They would appear to Westerners to be misshapen or unattractive. It is an important movement for us to consider because it shows what can happen when people shift their aesthetic. Anything can become game for collectors.

Collecting is a finely developed avocation in Great Britain, along with most things horticultural. Not only is the climate ideal for a wide variety of plants, but an expansive British Empire once offered endless opportunities for gathering them. There are other reasons that fuel this passion. England is far north and has a long, dark winter—colorful plants mean so much to people in that climate. Great Britain also has a very thin native plant pool due to island isolation and ice-age glaciation.

All of us who are collectors yearn to be the first to possess something like a variegated *Petasites* or a gold-leaf *Lysimachia* (moneywort). I love to acquire an unusual plant, but then I have to pass it along—the gift is precious yet affordable when the plant can be easily propagated. If it is a rare plant, I like to know that there will be just that many more opportunities for it to succeed.

If you ask rock gardener Budd Myers what his specialty is, he says plants of the Pennsylvania Shale, and he may be the only person focusing on this microhabitat. But a hunk of tufa rock—small enough to fit in a bathtub—gets most of the attention in his rock garden. Upon it, he has created the habitat of a windswept rock outcropping. A hundred tiny plants hug the crevices of this miniature landscape. One could spend days exploring this creation: planting, pruning, sweeping with a paintbrush.

The subjects of *The Collector's Garden* all have this kind of intensity and attention to detail. We see, hear, and smell volumes in every species.

INSIDERS' NETWORK

As I traveled around and met the most serious collectors, I was surprised to discover that most of these people knew one another, or had at least traded plants or communicated by phone or mail. Nearly everyone knows Jim Waddick (pages 153–55), although very few have ever met this proponent of old-fashioned letter writing. Nearly every insider seems to recognize the name Marco Polo Stufano (pages 209–15). His is probably the most-mentioned name of all.

I have tried to give Stufano plants over the years, but what do you give the man who has everything? Given the space constraints of Wave Hill, the public garden in the Bronx, New York, where Stufano is Director of Horticulture, a plant has to be pretty unusual or useful to become a resident. Marco usually tells me that he was already given this plant by so-and-so, or that plant by what's-his-name. Not only does everyone know of him, he also seems to know everyone, as well.

Panayoti Kelaidis, Curator of the Rock Garden at the Denver Botanic Garden, had a rare South African ice plant. One winter, the ice plant died and Kelaidis thought it was lost forever. Then, on a trip to the New York Botanical Garden, he saw it growing in a big pot. When he asked Robert Bartolomei, the curator of the rock garden, where he had found the plant that he believed to not exist anywhere in the world but in its tiny homeland, he was reminded that he had invited Bartolomei to take cuttings when he visited. Not only did it survive in New

OPPOSITE: *The cultivar* Robinia pseudo-acacia *'Frisia' made its way from the Netherlands to California to Vermont.* ABOVE: *Flowers of the familiar native species.*

York, but it turned out to be easy to grow. This succulent, when subjected to low light and heat, becomes wildly leggy, and one year it was used as scarecrow hair for a children's project. Kelaidis retrieved a piece to bring back to his garden and share with many friends.

Plant hoarding among collectors is common, but Kelaidis shares his plants, because every time he has tried to keep a plant to himself he has lost it. "Since I didn't pass it around," he says, "I don't have anyone to go to and get it back. It may even be lost forever." It might just be bad karma—hoarded treasures die. Panayoti Kelaidis is a born-again altruist who gets no greater thrill than sharing plants.

A plant can really get around. *Robinia pseudoacacia* is the common black locust native from Pennsylvania south to Georgia, west to Missouri and Oklahoma. It is rarely grown as an ornamental although it has luscious, fragrant, creamy-white flowers in mid to late spring in pendulous, grapelike clusters—typical of pea-family flowers like the wisteria's. There are many cultivated varieties, mostly from Europe, where these trees are sought after and respected. In the United States, they are generally considered weeds. There is a dark-pink-flowering one, *R. pseudoacacia* 'Purple Robe', and an ever-bloomer, *R. pseudoacacia* 'Semperflorens'.

The genus was named for Jean Robin (1550–1629), gardener to Henry IV of France. The species name means "false acacia," since the leaves resemble the mimosa, to which, in fact, this plant is related. Robin was the first to grow this American native in France in 1606. Three hundred years later, a gold-leafed form was discovered in an old nursery in Zwollerkerspel, Holland, and introduced in 1935 by W. Jansen.

Its chartreuse leaves hold their color through the growing season—especially in some shade. In full sun, they will darken to grass-green by summer's end. On cloudy or rainy days, it is an eye-catching ray of brightness. Although completely hardy, it is just beginning to catch on in the United States. Teen-aged trees occur in gardens in Vancouver and the coastal Pacific Northwestern States. In the East, we few who grow it are considered insiders. *Robinia pseudoacacia* 'Frisia' has had an erroneous cachet of rarity and cultural difficulty.

Wayne Winterrowd and Joe Eck have a few on their property in Vermont. The story of their plants shows how the insider's network works. Young plants from European cuttings were grown at Western Hills Nursery in California (pages 91–95). Winterrowd and Eck made a few attempts over the years to ship or bring plants home from California, and finally got one to grow.

I, too, have tracked this plant down for my garden. I found that Forest Farm (page 224) had small grafted plants. The next year, I found larger ones offered from Greer Gardens (page 223). Both of these nurseries are in Oregon. One from Forest Farm died; the other is about two stories tall. I am training the two from Greer over a metal

OPPOSITE: *The popular foliage and flower color combination of wine red and chartreuse is fostered by gardeners who trade varieties in these shades.* ABOVE: *Variegated horseradish* (Armoracia rusticana *'Variegata').*

arch in quite a bit of shade—a spectacular version of the golden arches. The leaves always move in the breeze and seem to shimmer. How long it will tolerate so much shade and being trained over an arbor is an open question— it wants to be a tree. I also wonder whether the species rootstock to which the tree was grafted will behave as it may in nature, sending up little plants from underground runners.

R. pseudoacacia 'Frisia' fits in well with the current design mania for combining chartreuse and burgundy foliage. At Western Hills, it grows in striking tandem with *Cotinus coggygria* 'Atropurpureus,' the purple smokebush. David Culp, the Chair of the Hardy Plant Society Mid-Atlantic Group, uses this color scheme at his garden in Pennsylvania. In 1994, he found a variegated ajuga with both these colors at Russell's Nursery. As the New York state sales representative for the wholesale herbaceous perennial nursery, Sunny Border, Culp often comes across plants developed or discovered by his clients and brings them back to go into production. In a few years, *Ajuga* 'Russell's Hybrid' will go beyond the insiders' network and find its way to your garden.

A variegated horseradish found its way to my garden from Wayne Winterrowd. This was a plant that Marco Polo Stufano actually wanted for Wave Hill. When mine started to fail from lack of sunlight, I offered it to him, and that's where it lives today. The network is alive.

BROKEN COLORS

We call the variation of foliage color *variegation*. Most trees and shrubs have colorful blooms for a couple of weeks. Herbaceous perennials might go on for a month or so. All gardeners, collectors or not, soon learn that foliage holds the garden together, and foliage color can spark areas whether in or out of bloom. Even among green leaves, there is more than just a single color. There are shades and tones: chartreuse, celadon, seafoam, verdigris, aquamarine, khaki—and park-bench-, jade-, bottle-, grass-, hunter-, olive-, lime-, emerald-, and forest-green. Leaves can display more than one color, as well—not merely with the flush of tender bright foliage in spring or fall—but throughout the growing season. Collectors thrill to tiny silver leaves or bronze ones, but little can excite the acquisition frenzy that leaves do with many colors all at once.

Just as there is more than one green, there's more to variegation than the typical white and green hosta. Bold bands or diffused mottling can combine green with one, two, three, four, or more shades. Bicolors, tricolors, quadricolors, and multicolors present brilliant yellow, orange, cream, white, salmon, pink, red, aubergine, gray, black, silver, or bronze. The markings also vary. There can be mottled blotches, geometric zones, zigzag edges, pointillistic dots, splashes, streaks, speckles, stripes, spots, sharply defined veins, or strokes of soft air-brushed color. Once considered clowns of the botanical world, variegated plants are now in vogue. More are coming on the market and growers seize any new entry and move it into production to feed the frenzy.

Variegated plants can be discovered in different ways. Sometimes, out of several thousand seedlings of a single species, one will display polychromatic foliage or flowers. Conversely, a normal-looking shrub or tree will for some reason push out a variegated shoot: a mutation, or sport.

There is sometimes concern among gardeners that variegation is caused by a virus that could spread to healthy plants. Dr. James Waddick (pages 153–55) dispells this fear. "There was a study at Cambridge University recently of 150 variegated plants. They found that in 99 percent of the cases, the variegation is not viral. It is chimeral and often very stable."

Chimeras are plants or plant tissues consisting of more than one genetic composition. In variegated leaves, mutation begins at a single point, and as the plant grows, both mutated and nonmutated cells are reproduced and distributed within the plant tissue—often side by side. The result could be that familiar green hosta with white margins.

In the beginning, give the variegated version of a plant the same sun exposure as its solid-colored counterpart, or a touch more. If the solid-green form of a plant needs shade, the variegate may want a little bit, too. If you're in doubt, start off by providing the required location for the nonvariegated version. Some variegation may be all but lost in deep shade. The exquisite white and green *Hemerocallis fulva* 'Kwanza Variegata' needs sun to keep its stripes.

Plants with little green chlorophyll need plenty of light to carry on photosynthesis since their food-producing areas are reduced. The striking variegated horseradish (*Armoracia rusticana* 'Variegata') has some leaves that are entirely white,

OPPOSITE: *The "broken" color of the clown fig* (Ficus aspera) *exemplifies the fascination of variegation.* ABOVE: Iris pallida *'Aurea Variegata' with* Helianthemum *flowers.*

without a speck of green, for example; and a pure white sport that appears as a branch of a shrub, will not make it on its own if an attempt is made to propagate and grow this albino curiosity.

The most treasured of all plants in Jim Murrain's garden in Missouri is the delicate and hard-to-grow version of an ordinarily noxious weed, *Polygonum cuspidatum* 'Variegatum.' "It's so variegated, it can barely stay alive," he says. "There's hardly enough chlorophyll for it to produce food." But it is a spectacular sight with buff-colored leaves brushed with pink, yellow, and salmon—a veritable sunset—on 5-foot-tall magenta stems.

Quirky and beautiful natural aberrations are fodder for the plant mill. In order to introduce these accidents to the public, nurseries have to reproduce them *vegetatively*—through stem cuttings or micropropagation (page 219).

The potential for a well-behaved variegate to become a weedy plant exists, because some plants, like a variegated Norway maple, may produce seeds that will revert to their original form and take over. It is unlikely that delicate harlequin cultivars will produce seed, but it is possible. The variegated barren strawberry (*Duchesnea indica* 'Variegata') could revert from the roots and turn into a vigorous spreader like its solid-green siblings.

Most problems with reversion are aesthetic. A variegated shrub may push out new shoots or watersprouts that are solid green. Remove them at once. In the case of a lilac or *Weigela,* there isn't an invasion threat, but the more vigorous solid-colored shoots will overpower and shade out the coloration for which you purchased the plant, and you'll be left with a rather ordinary specimen. Watch out for shoots that come up from the roots

ABOVE: Cornus florida *'Cherokee Sunset'* and Hosta *'Antioch' in the author's garden.* OPPOSITE, CLOCKWISE FROM TOP LEFT: *Variegated plants are often colorful turns on familiar ones, such as* Geranium phaeum *'Taff's Jester';* Hemerocallis fulva *'Kwanzo Variegata';* Impatiens *sp. (I. kew); a 2-foot-long leaf of the rare variegated rhubarb* (Rheum rhabarbarum *'Variegatum');* Hydrangea macrophylla *'Variegata'; blood banana* (Musa zebrina).

of some perennials during the growing season that might be solid green, and remove these as well.

Nancy Goodwin (pages 197–201), who collects hardy cyclamen, points out that every single sown seed of even one species (*Cyclamen hederifolium,* for example), produces a plant with distinctively individual leaf mottling. Just as in the case of rock-garden alpines, the small *Cyclamen* must be seen close up to be believed and appreciated.

Heavily patterned plants such as *Coleus hybridus* 'Flirtin' Skirts' with ruffled yellow, red, and green leaves, have markings that are so intricate, they too are best viewed at close range where their lively decoration can be enjoyed. (It should be noted that taxonomists are having their way with the genus *Coleus.* Like *Chrysanthemum,* there will be some divisions into newly named genera.) In Goodwin's North Carolina garden, large coleus plants create masses in containers in an outdoor-seating area. You sit in a chair and next to your elbow, just beyond a tall glass of iced tea, is a plant with a world of color in its busy leaves. The colors in this plant's variegation are echoed by its colorful companions—red *Euphorbia,* cream and green variegated impatiens, and orange begonia flowers.

Making a garden out of variegates is difficult. There is the compulsion to collect every one without consideration of the effect over all. In the case of the coleus, it would be a jittery nightmare. In a colorful flower or foliage border, consider treating such plants similarly to Goodwin's containerized specimens—as accents to define a theme—as stars. Use masses of solid-colored foliage plants on either side of the variegated collectable to make it stand out—isolated in all its glory.

OPPOSITE: *James deGrey David's garden in Texas relies on long-blooming annuals, such as orange cosmos and yellow zinnias, found in Mexico.* LEFT: Clematis florida 'Sieboldii', *named for Dr. Philipp Franz von Siebold (1791–1866), was among many plants found in Japan. Hunter John Tradescant the Younger (1608–1662) named* Tradescantia virginiana, ABOVE, *for his father, John the Elder (1570–1638).*

Hunters

When fifteenth-century explorers set off to find new worlds, they went in search not just of precious metals to stock the monarch's treasuries, but often in search of botanical gold: spices, medicinal herbs, fibers, and timber. Fame undoubtedly drove adventurers (as it does today), and the early plant hunters probably shared Sir Edmund Hillary's explanation for his quest to climb Mount Everest: "Because it was there."

Plant hunters, past and present, hope to discover an unknown form—a species of the genus they adore, a disease-resistant version of an imperiled botanical, or something entirely new that they may introduce, which will memorialize them in the plant's name. *Tradescantia virginiana*, for example, was named for the English explorer John Tradescant the Elder, who began one of Great Britain's gardening dynasties. His son, John Tradescant the Younger, found this plant, ubiquitous in the northeast United States, in Virginia during one of his trips to North America in the mid-1600s.

In some cases, an explorer sighted a wondrous plant, perhaps a botanical missing link, and others

THE COLLECTOR'S GARDEN

later organized a search party to bring back a specimen. There is also a certain amount of machismo in the thought of risking life and limb dangling from a cliff face to collect seed from a precious rock dweller; no surprise that most hunters have been male.

The great age of plant exploration waned at the end of the nineteenth century. But today, as more closed nations open up, we are in a new age of exploration, and many of the explorers come from the United States. Most of the headlines go to the discoverers of new animals, but the botanists have had the excitement of discovering plants that have immediate value to humanity. Scientists are feverishly cataloging endangered plants in places like Central America. One out of eight medicinal preparations in the Western world is derived from plants; the thousands of untested and still unknown plants may yield untold numbers of cures for diseases. The other driving force toward botanical discovery is the growing interest in gardening. In North America, hungry gardeners want new plants as fast as they can be introduced.

China has often been called "the Mother of Gardens," since its native flora has yielded so many plants for ornamental horticulture, including such favorites as tree peonies, oriental poppies, and camellias. Just a few years ago, someone asked present-day hunter Jim Waddick of Kansas City, Missouri, "Is there really anything left in China?" Since then, he has found previously unknown hostas and irises, hellebores, even trees. Americans like Waddick (pages 153–55), Barry Yinger (page 25), J. C. Raulston

Frittilaria persica, LEFT, *comes from high elevations in the Middle East; wild buckwheat,* RIGHT, *is from America's Rocky Mountains. Panayoti and Gwen Kelaidis (pages 161–62) know the importance of labels that include a plant's name* (Eriogonum ovalifolium) *and the source or site of seed collection.* OPPOSITE, BELOW: *The Western American native* Iris douglasiana *was named for hunter David Douglas (1798–1834).* OPPOSITE, ABOVE: *New colors of the popular rock garden subject,* Pulsatilla vulgaris (Anemone pulsatilla), *will be coming from the former Czechoslovakia.*

(page 63), Theodore Dudley, Daryl Apps, Lawrence Lee, and S. G. March are among the current leaders in the movement to get exotic plants into the nursery pipeline.

Cliff Davis, a professor at the University of North Carolina, specializes in woody plants, particularly beeches, and continues to make trips to China. He has brought back seeds of camellias and other new shrubs for the university, or to test in his home garden and offer through his family's mail-order and retail nursery, Camellia Forest.

Carl Schoenfeld and John Fairey of Texas (pages 31–37) stick a bit closer to home, making expeditions to Mexico. They find new plants on every trip and introduce the worthiest through botanical gardens and their own nursery, Yucca Do.

There are still many yet-to-be-discovered plants even in the United States. Plants of the *Fritillaria* genus include many intriguing species, few of which are known to gardeners. Among the places they are native are Greece, Turkey, Iran, Lebanon, Syria, Israel, Albania, and the former Yugoslavia. Interestingly, some species are indigenous to the western United States. Californian Wayne Roderick has made several discoveries, including February-blooming *Fritillaria biflora* 'Martha Roderick' (named for his mother by the Alpine Garden Society in London in 1990) in the foothills of the Sierra Nevada.

Scott Ogden searches West Texas for drought-tolerant plants that will also do well in difficult soil conditions. Gwen and Panayoti Kelaidis (pages 160–63) hunt for plants virtually in their own backyards—the steppes of the Rocky Mountains around Denver, Colorado. Panayoti Kelaidis has traveled the world, often visiting similar habitats in other countries such as Turkey and his ancestral home, Greece.

Dr. John Creech is an inspiration to contemporary hunters, too. He has led nine expeditions into the former Soviet Union and Eastern Asia. He was the Chief of the United States Department of Agriculture New Plants Research Branch and the Director of the National Arboretum in Washington, D.C., and has introduced countless woody plants.

There are plants to discover or rediscover practically everywhere. The Texas Rose Rustlers (pages 79–81) have been collecting old garden roses from yards, abandoned lots, and cemeteries for decades—a decidedly modern form of the collector's tradition.

Every day, species become extinct, but few come back from extinction. Wollemi pines were thought to be extinct for 50 million years, but in 1994, these relatives of the Norfolk Island pine were discovered in the Wollemi National Park in Australia. Twenty-three adults up to 130 feet tall and sixteen juveniles of this plant known previously only from fossils were found in a 1.2-acre tract of land in the 1.2-million-acre park near Sydney. Today, as centuries ago, the seduction of the hunt remains irresistible.

History

One of the earliest records of an organized plant-collecting venture was in Ancient Egypt, when Queen Hatshepsut dispatched hunters to gather live specimens of the source of myrrh (*Balsamodendron myrrha*) in 1495 B.C. Alexander the Great collected plants for Theophratus, the Greek philosopher and naturalist, and the Romans collected, as did every subsequent conquering empire. During the Renaissance, the Medicis sponsored collection trips.

Collection and colonization went together—the empires always explored to exploit the wealth of the conquered. Indeed many imported products have become associated with their destinations rather than their origins: cocoa with Holland, tomatoes with Italy, potatoes with Ireland. Medieval English monks gathered herbs as they traveled. In the Age of Exploration, the Spanish collected plants in Central and South America and, to a certain extent, in western North America. The French sent back plants from China, and later from North America, and the Dutch concentrated on the East Indies and Japan.

Most of the earliest introductions to the original North American colonies came from Europe, often with the English settlers. At first, the plants they brought were economic crops—food and medicinal plants. As the culture grew, the ornamentals, such as viburnums, lilacs, laurel, boxwood, heathers, heaths, and, of course, roses arrived.

Some of these immigrants, such as garden buttercups, thrived so well in their new homes that they became naturalized citizens growing in fields, marshes, and along the roadside. Some of the plants that seem quintessentially American are not indigenous at all: daisies, daylilies, and Queen-Anne's-lace, for example. Even the edible apple was imported by the settlers, who quickly cultivated 150 varieties.

In turn, the British brought back plants from the New World, including the potato, tobacco, corn, and sunflowers. The most influential transatlantic

Hunting, discovery, and introduction still go on today. Among the plants Roger Raiche (pages 43–47) found in California is Clarkia concinna ssp. raichei, LEFT. *Harold Epstein (pages 29–31) introduced the striped grass* Hakonechloa macra 'Aureola', ABOVE. *Some of our most popular plants came from East Asia, such as hosta (*H. 'Frances Williams'*) and astilbe, OPPOSITE.*

plant trader was Henry Compton, named bishop of London in 1675. The missionary John Banister also collected in Virginia, as did the scientist Mark Catesby, who later traveled south and wrote *Natural History of Carolina*.

Another collector in North America was Andre Michaux, who arrived from France in 1785. The explorations of Lewis and Clark also brought plants from across the continent, which was often treacherous work. Thomas Nuttall's name can be found in the species epithets of many Western natives such as *Cornus nutallii* (Pacific dogwood), as can the name of David Douglas.

The Royal Horticultural Society sent Douglas to the Northwest in 1825, and he spent most of his life collecting plants there. The shrub *Ribes sanguineum,* the flowering currant that is immensely popular in Europe, was his discovery, as were countless Western wildflowers such as *Eschscholzia californica* (California poppy), *Nemophila, Godetia,* as well as *Limnanthes douglasii* (meadow foam), just one of the plants that bears his name. The Douglas fir and the Douglas iris are his discoveries, too. Like so many hunters, he came to a tragic, if adventurous, end, gored to death by bulls in Hawaii.

One of the first nurseries in the colonies was begun by Robert Prince in Flushing, New York. Others followed as landowners began to develop estates in Virginia, Pennsylvania, and the Carolinas, and frequently imported plants via England, such as the Chinese camellias, to grow among the native oaks and magnolias.

China has played a big role in horticulture, but the opening of Japan in 1852 by Admiral Perry introduced what was probably the most important source of plants for North American gardens. The resource is so vast that it was not until the twentieth century that it was appreciated. Not only does Japan have more than 6,000 native trees to consider, but also the Japanese have an ancient history of cultivating ornamental plants.

Japan has similar habitats to the United States, too. Japanese woodlands produced pines and wild gingers, and many shrubs, including rhododendrons (evergreen azaleas) and hydrangeas—not so different from the mix in the United States. The same forests also yielded what became one of the most popular garden plants in the United States today—the hostas, arguably more popular in the United States than in their homeland. Recently, there has been a lot of interest in parallels between the plants of the eastern United States and those of Japan. The eastern United States is considered to be among the richest areas in plant diversity of the temperate world (second only to China), but there are some 90 United States genera that have analogous species in Japan. The list includes *Cornus florida*, our dogwood, and *C. kousa*, theirs; as well as many of the *Pachysandra, Hydrangea, Mahonia, Athyrium,* and *Hamamelis* genera.

Gardeners in the United States, with its diverse climates, have always had to be more selective than British gardeners, for example, who live in a welcoming moderate Zone 8. Still, there are many places around the world that have climates that are similar to one part of our country or another.

For warmer areas of North America, the Mediterranean region has been a popular source, but many of those plants came via British collectors. Tomorrow's favorites will come from Mexico, South Africa, Australia, and New Zealand. The last two countries are making conscious efforts to introduce their plants through commercial enterprises, because hunting can be big business.

The Arnold Arboretum Connection

Some of the test contributions to American horticulture were made with the help of Professor Charles Sprague Sargent, an aristocratic Bostonian who founded the Arnold Arboretum and was its director for fifty-four years. Between 1891 and 1902, he wrote the fourteen-volume work, *The Silva of North America*. The Sargent hemlock (*Tsuga canadensis* 'Pendula') is a glorious weeping form of our native—originally found in Beacon, New York, in 1870, and still treasured by landscape architects and designers. He traveled to Asia and discovered flowering cherry, *Prunus sargentii*, and crabapple, *Malus sargentii*, in the early 1890s. Perhaps Sargent's best acquisition was E. H. Wilson, who eventually became the Arnold's keeper and then Sargent's successor.

Ernest Henry Wilson was a student of the Royal College of Science at South Kensington, England, when the great British nurseryman Henry James Veitch engaged him to lead an expedition to collect seeds of the dove tree,

or handkerchief tree—*Davidia involucrata*—in China. The plant had been discovered by the missionary Père Jean-Pierre-Armand David, in 1866. Veitch's operation was huge, and he often employed as many as twenty hunters traveling around the world at one time. He suggested that Wilson visit Sargent on his way to China.

Sargent recommended that Wilson see Dr. Henry Augustine, a customs officer employed by the Chinese in Ichang, who had seen the dove tree. Augustine himself had discovered several plants including *Lilium henryi* and *Rhododendron augustinii*. Augustine witnessed the destruction of entire forests by the Chinese and was eager to promote plant hunting while there was still time. He gave Wilson a rough map of a large area where he recollected seeing the tree. Wilson finally located the area in 1900, but he discovered that the tree had been cut down for its wood.

When Wilson went to China, he was instructed to search only for the dove tree—there wasn't anything else of interest still there. Wilson found many other plants through his travels, however, up to the time he joined the staff of the Arnold Arboretum in 1927. He collected around 100,000 specimens of more than 5,000 species, and 60 plants were named for him. After first discovering a dove-tree relative, *Davidia laeta*, he finally did find the one he originally sought, *D. involucrata*, and collected its seed. Perhaps he is best known, though, for finding *Lilium*

Charles Sprague Sargent shaped the Arnold Arboretum by sponsoring plant exploration. Sargent is most associated with woody plants from China. He sent E. H. Wilson there to search for the legendary dove or handkerchief tree (Davidia involucrata), OPPOSITE. *Temperate areas of China have given us many plants, including the tree peony,* ABOVE. *New plants are coming from New Zealand, such as* Phormium tenax 'Purpureum', BELOW.

regale, the regal lily. "'Tis God's present to our gardens," he wrote. "Anybody might have found it, but—His whisper came to me."

Wilson survived hazardous trips to the Orient, including one when he broke a leg in a landslide. Sargent died in 1927, and Wilson succeeded him until 1930, when he and his wife were killed in a car accident. He was fifty-four years old.

The work at the Arnold continues today with hunters and curators such as Peter Del Tredici, Assistant Director for Living Collections, and Gary Koller, Senior Horticulturist. Arnold Arboretum is a member—along with several other United States institutions and a Canadian botanical garden—of the North American Plant Exploration Consortium. Organization members make yearly trips to China, so the tradition of Wilson is still alive.

THE YINGER GENERATION

Barry Yinger, one of the highest-profile modern hunters, thought he had met his end on more than one occasion: "I have fallen off rock faces, and come within an inch of being bitten by a deadly viper. But the closest call, I suppose, was when I was caught in a typhoon in the Yellow Sea. The motor of our little boat quit and we were being pushed toward the cliffs by the waves. I was trying to figure out who in the tiny boat I liked enough to save, when just at the last second, the motor started up and we got away."

Yinger has been interested in Asian plants since the sixth grade. "I was helping a lady with her garden and she explained that certain plants were found in both Asia and the part of the world that I was familiar with; they were related but different. Something just clicked."

He studied languages to get better information on the mysterious and often misunderstood Far Eastern cultures. The late Robert L. Baker, his professor at the University of Maryland, encouraged him, and shared a book called *Japanese Botany in the Age of the Wood Block Print* by Harley Harris Bartlett and Hide Shohara (University of Michigan). "It was the first time I ever saw cultivated *Asarum* [wild ginger]," says Yinger, "and it was a sort of an epiphany." He made his first trip to Asia in 1974, when as a college student he spent a semester in Japan. That sealed his fate. He has made forty trips since. Korea is the plant-hunting destination of the moment, since low winter temperatures will yield hardy species for American gardens.

Yinger believes that the future of horticulture

OPPOSITE: *One of hunter Barry Yinger's obsessions is the* Asarum *genus. He has seventy-five species, including* A. shuttleworthii. ABOVE: *Among the plants he sees for the future is the genus* Lespedeza.

lies in the hunt, because as gardeners mature, their hunger for unusual plants will increase. Demand will spur supply. "It's inevitable that some gardeners will ascend to an even higher plain," he says. "When people make a leap to the next level of appreciation, there have to be plants to satisfy that need. We don't have enough plants," he claims, predicting that horticulture is ready to make that leap.

"The typical gardener, years ago, just kept up with the neighbors. The typical garden-center customer today is someone asking what's new and what's better. You can see it with the variegated-plant people. They've gone beyond ornamental value to seek plants that are just bizarre; and then there are the people who collect mutations, and any curious conifers, cacti, or succulents. There will come a day when the cult of plants comes to K mart, Woolworth's, and Wal-mart. A couple of nurseries, such as We-du and Plant Delights, know this. It's coming."

Yinger now collects and develops plants for his employer, a visionary plant wholesaler. His latest passion is for the bush clovers, *Lespedeza* spp. He has about forty selections, and is concentrating on these semiwoody, leguminous plants used in Japan to improve soil. People here grow them as if they were herbaceous, cutting them to the ground in spring. Late in the growing season, they produce oceans of tiny pealike flowers in shades from red to pink to white. "They're a good example of some of the new things coming on the market," he says. "They will fill a void for American gardeners—color in late summer and early fall—sparse times for blossoming shrubs."

25

HUNTERS

THE FATHER OF COLLECTORS

The largest collection efforts in the British American colonies were carried out by an American-born colonist: John Bartram (1699–1777). His contributions, not only to the riches of his Anglican ancestral home, but to North American horticulture, are lasting. Modern collectors will recognize a kindred spirit in the man who developed the nation's first botanical garden.

It was also a nursery that supplied many plants to George Washington's Mount Vernon home. In Kingsessing, near Philadelphia, Bartram began his collection in 1729. Between 1736 and 1766 he traveled to the Carolinas, Connecticut, Florida, Georgia, Maryland, New Jersey, New York, and Virginia in search of plants. He fortunately had patrons, or subscribers, in England who funded his expeditions, and they each received a box of seeds of about one hundred different plants for their fee. Bartram's discoveries soon found their way to many British gardens.

The hundred years or so spanned by the activity of Bartram and his fourth son and successor, William, are known as the naturalists' period, when there was a great interest in explaining the natural world. The goal was to establish a hierarchy of living things and to discover and fill in the missing links. In 1753, Carolus Linnaeus of Sweden (1707–1778) published *Systema Plantarum,* the method of classifying all living things with binomial nomenclature (two names), which remains the basis for taxonomy today. Linnaeus called John Bartram "the world's greatest natural botanist."

William Bartram's patron was Dr. John Fothergill, for whom the native shrub *Fothergilla* was named. In 1783, the younger Bartram published a catalog—the nation's first—listing more than 200 plants. Among the Bartrams' introductions were: arborvitae, birch, Carolina allspice, elm, fringe tree, redbud, Kentucky coffee tree, larch, magnolia, oakleaf hydrangea, pawpaw, rhododendron, sumac, sweet gum, and viburnum. Discoveries of herbaceous treasures such as Venus flytrap, shooting star, and lady's-slipper orchid created an unparalleled list.

John Bartram started the first botanical garden in North America on the site of his house in Kingsessing, Pennsylvania, ABOVE. *He and his son William traveled throughout the colonies finding plants such as oakleaf hydrangea* (Hydrangea quercifolia), OPPOSITE.

After a visit in 1754, Bartram's young friend Dr. Alexander Garden wrote: "His garden is a perfect portraiture of himself, here you meet with a row of rare plants almost covered over with weeds, here a beautiful shrub, even luxuriant amongst briars, and in another corner an elegant and lofty tree lost in a common thicket. In a word he disdains to have a garden less than Pennsylvania, and every den is an arbor, every run of water a canal, and every small level spot a parterre, where he nurses up some of his idol flowers and cultivates his darling productions."

Who among us has not visited such a place, perhaps a shaggy nursery where among the ruins are the most precious discoveries, or maybe this is our own garden? We collectors are all the descendants of John Bartram.

27

HUNTERS

It must be the dream of every gardener to have what Harold Epstein has earned: the chance to see his plants grow to maturity. Most people move around so much that few of us can plant a tree seed or seedling and sit in the shade that it eventually casts. Harold and Esta Epstein moved to their Westchester, New York, house on 1½ acres in the spring of 1937. Today, many of the original hemlocks, rhododendron, mountain laurels, and dwarf maples live in the garden where Epstein still works with the woman who has been his talented assistant for over thirty years, Lois Himes.

Among the rarities Epstein has successfully grown is dawn redwood, *Metasequoia glyptostroboides*, a tree known only from fossil records and thought to be extinct until it was rediscovered in western China in 1941. Planted as a seedling in the spring of 1950, Epstein's specimen is now close to 100 feet tall.

Harold Epstein is the elder statesman of the modern collectors in America. His garden is home to thousands of hardy plants gathered on trips to Europe and Asia. Eastern United States natives are here too, though about three-quarters of his plants come from Japan. There is an analogous species theme in this garden—cousins, as it were—that plays out with parallel Asian and American versions of plants. Such relatives include members of the genera: *Arisaema, Jeffersonia, Maianthemum, Asarum, Rhododendron,* and *Polygonatum.*

Most amazing to me is the tiny *Epimedium,* or barrenwort. *E.* × *youngianum* 'Niveum' has become Epstein's signature plant, and a small one installed fifty years ago along the edge of rock steps still grows in a large but tidy clump. These low, semievergreen ground covers are easy to grow and have few

Harold Epstein has inspired hundreds of collectors, especially rock gardeners, through his exemplary quest for unusual plants. OPPO-SITE: *His mature garden, near New York City, is home to many of these plants, specifically ones from Japan such as,* ABOVE, LEFT TO RIGHT, *a rare variegated fairy bells,* Disporum sessile *'Albo Marginata',* Paeonia obovata *'Alba', and* Arisaema sikokianum, *one of the plants for which he is known.*

pest or disease problems. His *Epimedium* collection, probably the largest in North America, includes several he collected in China, notably *E. sagitatum,* which is used as an herbal birth control in its native land.

The site is dominated by huge granite outcroppings, but rather than letting them obstruct his garden plan, Epstein created a naturalistic landscape from the boulders, even relocating others from outlying parts of the property, creating one big rock garden.

Early on each year, the *Corylopsis pauciflora* blooms if the winter has been kind. Then deciduous and evergreen azaleas such as the Japanese royal azalea or *Rhododendron schlippenbachii* carry on, with *Enkianthus* species (ericaceous, *Rhododendron* relatives), and *Kerria japonica.* Epstein is thinking about introducing a new *Kerria* with exceptionally large single flowers and a vigorous upright growth-habit more like the double-flowered *K. japonica* 'Pleniflora' than the species.

He is also known as a collector of dwarf woody plants, including smaller versions of *Enkianthus* and *Rhododendron. Enkianthus* are also prized for brilliant fall color. The most amazing in Epstein's garden and rarest of all is a very compact form of *E. perulatus.* "After fifty years, it is only two feet tall and about as wide—you'll never see anything like it," he says.

Thirty years ago, Epstein collected *Anemone trifolia* in northern Italy, on a trip with Esta, and *Hosta minor* is another of his treasures, brought back from the coast of Korea. Still, after more than sixty years of seeking out fine subjects, many of his favorite plants have not found their way into American gardens.

One introduction, however, is very popular today. After a quarter century in his garden, *Hakonechloa macra* 'Aureola', a spectacular, well-behaved golden grass, finally succeeded. Epstein also grows the rarely seen solid-green form; but it is unlikely that anyone will ever discover the beauty he sees in this species—it is as unassuming as its protector.

The more open area of the garden features a grass lawn among large rock outcroppings, ericaceous *plants such as* Enkianthus *and* Rhododendron, *and the genus for which Epstein is most famous*—Epimedium. *Some are named cultivars, such as* E. cantabrigense *that hugs the rock,* OPPOSITE. *Others are hybrids that have occurred in the garden:* ABOVE LEFT, *A dwarf* E. grandiflorum; CENTER, E. × youngianum *'Roseum'; and* RIGHT, E. grandiflorum *'Violaceum' seen with white* Anemone blanda.

W hen most gardeners consider the origins of exotic plants for gardens, they probably first think of the Far East, where hostas, daylilies, and countless conifers originated. Perhaps then comes the rest of Asia and Europe. West Coast gardeners point to Australia, South Africa, South America, and New Zealand. Few people would think of a place much closer to home, but even before the NAFTA trade agreement simplified importation, a select group of pioneers were looking toward Mexico as a plant source.

With a topography that boasts both deserts and mountains, Mexico yields plants for many gardens in many climates. Its offerings include some that send collectors into a frenzy of desire: a dogwood, *Cornus florida* ssp. *urbiniana,* with bluish leaves, pink petioles, and recurved white bracts that nearly form a globe; and several mountain bee balms, including scarlet *Monarda schiedeana* that may, someday, be part of many perennial borders—even as far north as USDA Zone 6.

Several of these discovered by John Fairey and Carl Schoenfeld since 1988 have become the focal points in their Texas garden and the focus of their mail-order nursery, Yucca Do, offering more than 150 plants of Mexican origin. "We specialize in plants from Mexico—ones adapted to the drought of the desert and the cold of the mountains," says Schoenfeld. "Few people realize that there are many plants that are not unlike familiar ones here." Most of the ones they propagate are for USDA Zones 7–9.

ABOVE: *One area of John Fairey and Carl Schoenfeld's garden features an artwork-in-progress—a long blue wall—with plant discoveries from Mexico that the men will introduce through their nursery.* OPPOSITE: Manfreda sileri *and* M. undulata *in bud stand tall in front of the fuzzy new growth of* Ipomopsis rubra *(standing cypress) and spiky* Yucca rostrata.

The search for a diversity of plants suitable for the hot and humid climate of Central Texas led Schoenfeld and Fairey to accompany retired nurseryman Lynn Lowery, in July 1988, on a trip to Northern Mexico to collect seeds and cuttings. Their lives changed. "During that four-day trip, we saw growing conditions ranging from high-altitude cloud forest to desert," says Fairey.

And the fact that so many plants were found in the mountains makes them surprisingly hardy—something one does not expect from the southernmost country in North America. The collecting would begin early in the morning and continue by flashlight well into the night. Lowery knew nearly everything about Mexican and Texan flora, and how to obtain permits on both sides of the border. He also shared his expertise on cleaning, storing, and germinating seed.

On their third expedition, they were determined to see the unusual plants of the Sierra Chiquita, where forests cover the mountains at about 3,400 feet, and the climate is dry in the summer and quite cold in winter. They found themselves in forests of *Acer, Abies, Carya, Carpinus, Ostrya, Quercus, Taxus, Viburnum, Cercis, Cornus,* and two species of *Ilex.* There they discovered *Ilex rubra,* an impressive holly with glossy, serrated leaves, and large red fruits more than a ¼ inch in diameter.

The woody plants are among their most exciting finds. *Clethra pringlei* 'White Water', an evergreen summersweet, can reach 25 feet and has fragrant flowers that smell of cinnamon. In 1988 in the mountains just east of Mamulique Pass—70 miles from Texas, at altitudes of 4,000 to 5,000 feet, they collected a small quantity of *Ceanothus* seed that eventually produced four plants. They selected one with fragrant flowers in a deeper blue than any they had seen in Mexico and named it *Ceanothus coeruleus* 'Azure Mist'.

Acer skutchii is a sugar maple with pink new foliage that deepens to red and fall foliage in yellow and

ABOVE LEFT: *A pride and joy among Yucca Do's many new introductions is an evergreen, long-blooming wine cup,* Callirhoë involucrata *'Tenuissima'. Plants in the collections throughout the property include bear grass,* ABOVE RIGHT, Nolina longifolia, *and,* OPPOSITE, Brahea armata, *a palm selected for its silver-blue fronds.*

orange not unlike the northern sugar maple. A *Carpinus* species (hornbeam) is still unidentified. But it is very different from familiar ones with pendant branches and new growth of bronze-pink.

Schoenfeld and Fairey also saw countless evergreen oaks, *Quercus* species. These are very interesting not only for their varied leaf shapes and growth habits, but also because they seem to be resistant to oak decline, so they might become replacements for trees in the South and West, where shade trees are so important, and many oaks are failing.

Some of the best herbaceous and semievergreen plants introduced by Yucca Do include a new species of the bulb *Zephyranthes*—a floriferous rain lily with pink flowers found growing in the rich humus among house-sized granite boulders—*Zephyranthes* 'Labuffarosa'. It is easy to grow from seed and reaches blooming size in three to four years. In all their travels, they have never seen it again.

Among the fifty-four kinds of *Salvia* offered in the Yucca Do catalog is *S. blepharophylla* 'Sweet Numbers'. It has large red flowers on 15-inch stems, appearing on and off all summer.

If Fairey and Schoenfeld have a favorite of the moment of all their introductions into cultivation, it is a poppy mallow, *Callirhoë involucrata* 'Tenuissima' (Zones 6–9), an evergreen ground cover with pale violet flowers. Unlike our native wine cup, which becomes dormant in the summer, this one continues to flower through spring and into August.

The mission: to get these plants into cultivation. To that end, Fairey and Schoenfeld have donated seed or cuttings to the National Arboretum in Washington, D.C., North Carolina State Arboretum in Raleigh, the University of California at Berkeley and Santa Cruz, the Arnold Arboretum in Massachusetts, Mereweather Arboretum in Australia, Chollipo Arboretum in South Korea, and the Royal Botanic Gardens at Kew in England—a list almost as impressive as the Yucca Do catalog itself.

OPPOSITE: *In 1990, Fairey and Schoenfeld found* Echeveria shaviana *in the wild. Now these blue-green succulents with coral flowers grow in stone pots under a pergola by the house.* ABOVE: *Another cool view of the garden with the excellent Louisiana iris 'Southern Lady' and the pergola in the background.*

Dr. Nick Nickou, a retired general practitioner, has the largest collection of species *Rhododendron* in New England, but his Connecticut property also features one of the best collections of woody plants anywhere, including *Enkianthus, Magnolia, Acer,* and *Daphne* species and varieties, and such herbaceous curiosities as an enormous *Arisaema ringens,* numerous ferns, countless alpines, and what has been touted as a dwarf ginkgo.

Nickou has a reputation as an itinerant collector. He takes two trips out of the country a year and has been to Greece six times, twice to Turkey, and twice to the Himalayas. He has visited Iceland and Greenland, Spain, Russia, and the Alps, and collected forty-nine species in Western China. He has bred some plants and is especially interested in experimenting with ferns. *Athyrium* × 'Branford Beauty', a cross he made from the Japanese painted fern and the native red-stalked lady fern, is now commercially available.

His garden, in turn, has become a significant source of plants for home gardens, mostly through the efforts of Phil Waldman of Roslyn Nursery, in Dix Hills, New York, who for fifteen years has collected from Nickou's 3-acre garden.

Pushing the limit of plant hardiness is another dimension of Nickou's collection. It often gets to 10 or more degrees F below 0, but quite a few of its inhabitants are not rated that hardy. Not only are the plants arranged beautifully, they are also sited to simulate their climatic preferences. *Crinum* × *powellii,* a lily usually grown outdoors only in Florida, has thrived in a protected area for twenty-five years. They dependably send up around eight pink fragrant flowers each in late summer to fall by a south-facing wall where the house stores heat and the ground never freezes.

Nick Nickou specializes in Rhododendron *in gardens on seven acres.* ABOVE LEFT: *The garden slopes down to the front door, where an enormous specimen of the hybrid 'Scintillation' blooms.* ABOVE RIGHT: Rhododendron *species, hybrids, and cultivars are tucked into pockets all around the property, punctuating a remarkable collection that includes vines such as the kiwi fruit relative,* Actinidia kolomikta, OPPOSITE. *Some of the leaves of the male plants seem dipped in white or pink paint.*

Nickou's massive clump of *Arisaema ringens,* a favorite of many collectors in this book, is more than 3 feet across—a sensational specimen. The *Camellia japonica* 'Kumasaka', an 8-foot evergreen by the front door, breaks the rules of hardiness, too. Far from wrapping it each winter, Nickou does nothing to protect it (or any plant) beyond choosing a good location.

The list of tender subjects goes on: shrubs such as Asian *Rhododendron discolor, R. pentaphyllum,* and *R. quinquefolium,* and *Clethra barbinervis,* a rare summer sweet with fragrant lacy white flowers that Nickou has trained into a tree. *Illicium floridanum* (Florida anise) confirms my suspicion as to its actual hardiness. This wonderful and rarely seen American native blooms perfectly at Nickou's with a 1½-inch-wide wine-red flower that looks much like the seedpod of its relative, the star anise, or a small passion flower. His *Daphne* species, pressed into the cold, are spectacular. Most *Daphne* species are hardy enough, but *D. tangutica* from Northwest China, and *D. retusa,* which Nickou admired in the wilds of Sichuan, are not. Still, in this garden, they blossom. *D. retusa* presents its tubular white-tinged violet flaring flowers and *D. tangutica,* white-blushed pink. *D. cneorum* produces fragrant, rose-purple flowers in dense clusters at the ends of the branches in early spring, and *D. genkwa* has lilac, faintly fragrant blossoms.

Nickou grows the extremely unusual wheel tree, *Trochodendron aralioides,* which, according to woody plant expert Michael Dirr, "is a virtual unknown in American gardens, but occasionally appears—like Brigadoon—in collections." *Trochodendron* is only supposed to be hardy in Zone 8, but so many woody plants, from *Aucubas* to *Zenobia,* grow at Nickou's, whether they are supposed to or not.

Nickou takes great pleasure in fooling Mother Nature, and just about anybody. He has a wonderful sense of humor and is not at odds with playing a horticultural prank on the unsuspecting visitor. "Have you seen my dwarf ginkgo?" He shows it with pride, telling of countless visitors startled at this shrub less than 12 inches tall in its twentieth year. "I prune it back to a stump every spring. It fools everyone."

ABOVE LEFT: *An expansive rock garden, surrounded by low stone retaining walls, dominates the front yard. Magnificent blossoming woody specimens, including the white-flowered* Magnolia × wieseneri (M. watsonii), ABOVE RIGHT, *are placed throughout the property.* OPPOSITE, CLOCKWISE FROM TOP LEFT: Enkianthus campanulatus *'Showy Lanterns';* Clematis ochroleuca; Arisaema ringens; *Nickou's own development,* Athyrium × *'Branford Beauty', a hybrid of the Japanese painted fern* (A. niponicum *'Pictum') and the native lady fern* (A. filix-femina).

The inspiration for Roger Raiche's garden in Berkeley, California, is nature. Every evening after leaving the University of California at Berkeley Botanical Garden, where he is a horticulturist, he works in his own yard until nightfall. He looks like a mountain climber and scampers through the place with the energy and strength one would associate with an adventurous athlete. In fact, Raiche does a lot of hiking and climbing—nearly every weekend—when he searches for new plants. In an era when even active naturalists are content to check off entries in their nature guides rather than hunt for unknown varieties, Raiche is a rarity. Even more remarkable is that the hills and mountains around San Francisco actually do have unknown plants for him to discover.

Raiche has introduced over a dozen native California plants to horticulture. Some of these are not just botanical curiosities, but extraordinary garden plants. Four plants bear his name: *Arctostaphylos stanfordiana* ssp. *raichei* is a manzanita he discovered. *Calochortus raichei* is a challenging member of the Mariposa lily genus with nodding globular flowers resembling "art nouveau street lamps," he says. The small-horned subspecies of *Clarkia concinna* was named *raichei* for its discoverer, too, and is everblooming. (The original *Clarkia* was found by earlier explorers and hunters, Lewis and Clark.) Among the selections he has made are *Vitis californica* 'Roger's Red', an ornamental grape that turns bright red in the fall, and he also recently found a red-leafed strain of the orchid, *Epipactis gigantea,* which he is calling 'Serpentine Night'.

43

H
U
N
T
E
R
S

OPPOSITE: *Roger Raiche gardens on a small plot of land around the studio of the late California architect Bernard Maybeck. He shares the garden with designer Tom Chakas, whose steep "Mediterranean Hillside" can be seen in the distance.* ABOVE: *Raiche, inspired by the California hills—even the abandoned mines—dyed chunks of found concrete a rust color to make a bench.*

In private life, Raiche gardens on the land surrounding his rented house—once the studio of the late Bernard Maybeck, the influential architect of the California Arts and Crafts Movement. His housemate is the garden designer Tom Chakas (page 106). Raiche's areas are filled with unusual plants—not natives exclusively, although he oversees the Eastern Native Plant collection and the California collection at the University of California Botanical Garden. In his home garden, natives mingle with exotics. Raiche is an artist as well as a hunter, and selection is made for aesthetic reasons, but the inspiration for the garden is the wild, or more precisely, the indigenous landscape. This part of California is a grassland, and although it has a kind of lushness in spring, it receives only about 20 to 30 inches of rainfall a year.

Raiche has included many spiky, architectural plants, such as *Phormium*, yucca, and iris, and an equal number of airy, frothy ones that are unceasingly animated. "I love the way the grasses and other paniculate plants are backlit in the afternoon," he says, "it's one of my favorite times. They glisten." He refers to the sparkling flowers of *Macleaya cordata*, plume poppy, a dwarf *Thalictrum isopyroides*, and a host of grasses including a spectacular native bunch grass that Raiche introduced, *Calamagrostis foliosa*. Another species, *Stipa gigantea*, has the largest flowers of any grass. "I love to show this plant to people. You can really see the botanical structure of the inflorescence."

Several areas of the property have names: Helictotrichon Hill is named for the silvery-green grass that lines its path; Chakas calls his steep garden Mediterranean Hillside for its terrain and plants—reminiscent of that region. The lower garden by the lawn is called the "Head-in-the-Hole Garden," where a carved stone face by Marcia Donahue (pages 203–207) rests in a depression in the paving.

ABOVE LEFT: Brugmansia × *'Charles Grimaldi'* (Datura *hybrid*). ABOVE RIGHT: Phormium cookianum *'Tricolor'*.
OPPOSITE, CLOCKWISE FROM TOP LEFT: *An earthquake-proof pot holder made of another favorite material—rebar; Tom Chakas plants the containers on the patio with specimens such as the vertical umbrella palm* (Cyperus alternifolius) *growing in water in the large pot and silver-leafed* Euphorbia myrsinites; *at "Sulphur Springs," Raiche created another allusion to the mines with a surprisingly odoriferous element—he adds sulphur to the fountain's water; many materials, such as the sink in the "Head-in-the-Hole Garden" and paving recycled from post-earthquake freeway rubble, find their way here.*

On the other side of Mediterranean Hillside is a place where Raiche has let his artistic imagination run wild. "I have always been fascinated by the old abandoned mines that you see in the hills," he says. And so he started to construct the Rust Patio, a bench and steps made out of discarded concrete pieces, soaked and stained with iron sulfate powder. More iron is creeping into the garden in the form of rebar (steel reinforcing rods used in concrete construction) twisted into shapes that line the path leading up the hill. "We have a terrible deer problem—not from eating as much as from running through the garden. So I put up these pieces of iron to guide them through. It works." Raiche has also made some interesting spiral holders for precious urns to make them earthquake-proof.

The number of different species and cultivars in the collection is unfathomable—especially in such concentration. In creating this garden, Raiche admits that he has learned a lot about plants. He is completely aware of the breadth of his achievement, but it's hard to get a sense of who is master. Often he talks of how the garden suggested this, or the garden wanted that. It seems, in the end, to be a collaboration. It would be easy to imagine that Raiche was a plant in a former life.

OPPOSITE: *The hill to the road is a subtle study in color and texture with bearded iris, white rock rose, California poppies, and the ever-moving grasses.* ABOVE: *Light and movement are always on Raiche's mind and many plants are arranged to take advantage of the setting sun as well as the breeze coming up into the hills of Berkeley. A somewhat unconventional foundation planting of mostly herbaceous plants hugs fast to the studio, where they catch the last embers of the sun setting over San Francisco.*

OPPOSITE: *Mount Cuba Center for the Study of the Piedmont Flora is not only a beautiful garden, but has a mission: to introduce, promote, conserve, and disseminate native plants from the Mid-Atlantic region.* ABOVE: *One of their introductions—a goldenrod cultivar, 'Golden Fleece'.* LEFT: *The rare blue Himalayan poppy* (Meconopsis betonicifolia) *is started from seed donated by plant society members—one of the best ways to acquire plants.*

Missionaries

Some collectors are born-again sorts who feel the need to spread the word about their passion with evangelical zeal. The ardor of these missionaries goes beyond possession of a plant. They mount enthusiastic crusades for varying reasons with various goals—but primarily to gain converts to their way of thinking or seeing. Missionaries have a profound belief in the power of plants, and they are convinced that you would see it, too, if you would just allow yourself to be converted.

They might be botanical garden curators eager to exhibit a specific genus and educate the public. They could be like Dan Hinkley (pages 71–77), of Kingston, Washington, who chose the nursery industry as the method to distribute his favorite plants. Some, like Norman Singer and Geoffrey Charlesworth (pages 87–89), work through the North American Rock Garden Society to communicate their passion. Singer and Charlesworth also proselytize using the power of propagation, and practice what they preach—sowing seeds of some 3,000 different plants each year.

Some missionaries are teachers who influence hundreds of students to go into the world of horticulture or to venture in search of new and better botanicals. Teachers like Fred Case (pages 67–69), J. C. Raulston (page 63), and Hal Bruce, the late Curator of Plants at Winterthur Museum and Gardens, in Winterthur, Delaware, publish inspiring books and articles, and lecture around the country. Raulston also, literally, makes plants available to nurseries. At the North Carolina State University Arboretum, his active program of dissemination offers cuttings to commercial growers.

Brent Heath (pages 103–104), owner of the Daffodil Mart in Gloucester, Virginia, knows everything about *Narcissus* species and cultivars and lectures on these spring-flowering bulbs and others. He is spreading the word not only about his favorite plants, but also about his mail-order bulb business. Direct-mail growers can be missionaries, too.

Sometimes the mission is to more than get the word out—it is to save the world, or at least a little corner of it. Some people who collect are moved by the desire to preserve and conserve plants. They never collect endangered species from the wild to grow in zoolike gardens; they rescue plants from threatened habitats; and they operate very active propagation programs to make more of these plants available to botanical gardens, growers, and gardeners—new homes for the endangered exotics or natives.

Dr. Richard Lighty of Mount Cuba Center for the Study of the Piedmont Flora, in Delaware, a beautiful private estate garden owned by Mrs. Lammot DuPont Copeland that is also an institution dedicated to the promotion of the native plants of the Piedmont, works to bring garden-worthy selections of indigenous plants to the nursery industry. Mike Shoup (pages 79–81), of the Antique Rose Emporium, in Brenham, Texas, propagates old garden roses that have been discovered in cemeteries and abandoned properties and backyards in the South, and helps to ensure that these plants will not only persist but be grown in more gardens all over the country.

Barry Glick has been instrumental in propagating eastern North American indigenous plants. His nursery, Sunshine Farms in Renick, West Virginia, offers many southeastern native plants—eight different trillium, for example. All plants are *nursery propagated*—the key phrase for determining an ethical source for wildflowers. He has been collecting for about a quarter century and building a garden on 60 acres on a mountaintop 3,000 feet above sea level.

"My collection numbers well over 10,000 different taxa," says Glick. Many are rare and come from imminently endangered habitats. But he is, first and foremost, a collector of collectors. His mission is to create a clearinghouse for private collections in North America and make sure that they will be preserved beyond the lives of their guardians. In 1991, he started a group called the North American Plant Preservation Council modeled after England's National Council for the Conservation of Plants and Gardens. Unlike the American Association of Botanical Gardens and Arboreta (AABGA), which tracks collections in public institutions, Glick's new society will be dedicated to private ones.

The missionaries all propagate. Norman Singer and Geoffrey Charlesworth (pages 87–89) start seeds of 3,000 different plants every year. Seeds are potted on the bench outdoors and carefully watered—a deceptively bucolic undertaking until in short order thousands of pots fill cold frames around the property. The contents of one is shown in detail, OPPOSITE.

Eventually, when the number of listed collectors reaches about 200, Glick will reveal who they are and where their collections are located in a published directory, but for now, most of that information remains confidential. A few early members, however, include Dr. W. George Schmidt of Tucker, Georgia, who has nearly 1,000 hosta cultivars, and Polly Hill of Martha's Vineyard, Massachusetts, the great woody plant breeder, who has among her charges a large *Stewartia* collection.

The great American botanical gardens all have collections, as described in the AABGA's plant collections directory (page 239). Many preserve the gene plasma of endangered plants and provide an opportunity for the public to see rare plants and learn about them for their gardens—maybe even get hooked on a particular genus.

Some accomplish their mission by being a visual inspiration either as a living museum of plants or as an aesthetic showcase for them. At Wave Hill in the Bronx, New York (pages 209–15), there are always visitors making their way through the Flower Garden with notebooks in hand, jotting down Latin names and recording plant combinations. The same is true of the rock garden at the Denver Botanical Garden.

Where to Find Plants

Botanical gardens are great places to buy plants as well. Most have gift shops, but the real secret is to go to sales and auctions, such as those held at Strybing Arboretum and Botanical Gardens, in San Francisco, California, and at Missouri Botanical Garden, in St. Louis, Missouri. At the yearly auction of the New York Botanical Garden, plants propagated by staff members are for sale. Some of the best ones are from the native plant collections and are rarely offered on the market.

The granddaddy of plant auctions is the one held yearly at Longwood Gardens, in Kennett Square, Pennsylvania, to raise money for the Delaware Center for Horticulture. The newest plants on the market come through the silent auction tables at this event. The tale is always told of Sir John Thouron's pale yellow-flowered *Clivia miniata*. The first year one was put up for auction, it was rumored to have brought $10,000. The truth is that it went for $1,700, but that is still quite a sum for a houseplant.

One year I found myself bidding for a lot of five gold-leafed Boston ivies, *Parthenocissus tricuspidata* 'Fenway'. (This golden treasure was found growing on the fence at Boston's Fenway Park.) I won the bid, but afterward, someone asked me if I knew who it was that I was feverishly bidding against. It was a

descendant of the affluent family who built Longwood. I sent her one of the plants and shared the others with friends.

The Arnold Arboretum, just outside of Boston, Massachusetts, lies on about 340 acres of what was originally rolling farmland, which was transformed into an arboretum with money bequeathed by Hames Arnold in 1872. Charles Sprague Sargent was appointed curator and persuaded Frederick Law Olmsted to lay out the grounds. Sargent's mandate was to sponsor collecting around the world and to grow and introduce new plants.

The Arnold is still a collector's garden. Among the unrivaled collections of tree and shrub specimens is its famous collection of lilacs. Nearly all the lilacs in most gardens are varieties of *Syringa vulgaris,* so it really is astounding to visit the Arnold on Lilac Day and see thirty-two distinct species among the four hundred varieties in the collection.

Not all botanical collections are on the mighty scale of the Arnold Arboretum. Don Jacobs, who has a Ph.D. in ecology and has taught at the University of Georgia, is a plant hunter who has traveled through China, Japan, Taiwan, Singapore, Europe, and most of North America. He founded Eco-Gardens in Decatur, Georgia, a botanical collection amassed for the research and display of native and exotic plants of the Southeast. Jacobs's collection is designed to exhibit plants and also to supply these to botanical gardens. This is not a megabusiness, but fortunately for us, he sells the overflow to the public to help sustain the nursery and gardens. His list is outstanding—varied, eclectic, and esoteric. Jacobs sells more *Arisaema* species and relatives than does any other United States nursery.

Direct-mail growers make it possible for us to get an astounding variety of plants from all over the

Missionaries dream of discovering and introducing new plants, such as Parthenocissus tricuspidata *'Fenway',* ABOVE LEFT, *a gold Boston ivy found climbing a wall at Fenway Park. The Arnold Arboretum exhibits plants that can grow locally, such as lilac 'Katherine Havemeyer',* ABOVE RIGHT. OPPOSITE: Baptisia arachnifera *is an endangered species that Tony Avent has permission to propagate.*

world delivered right to our doorsteps. (See Mail-order Nurseries.) There are wonderful mail-order nurseries catering to the collector, and more people are getting involved in this labor of love all the time. Since nurseries have limited room to grow the plants, mail-order seed catalog companies fill in the gap. There are up to two million begonia seeds to the ounce, for example, so a purveyor can easily store a billion seeds in a household refrigerator. As an individual collector, you can order seeds for a thousand plants—all for the cost of buying and shipping a few perennials from one rare-plant nursery or a small tree from the local garden center. All the great collectors have mastered the skill or art of propagation, especially from seeds—the most efficient means of transporting genetic material.

Panayoti and Gwen Kelaidis (pages 161–63) start tens of thousands of tiny rock-garden plants in what used to be their driveway in a Denver suburb. Panayoti Kelaidis can pot up 1,500 seedlings in a single weekend. It is his "Zen therapy," he says. The plants that are grown may ultimately be sold at fund-raisers for the Denver Botanical Garden, where Panayoti Kelaidis is rock-garden curator, or by the local chapter of the North American Rock Garden Society; given to friends; or very often, used as the resource for the Kelaidises' seed nursery, Rocky Mountain Rare Plants.

Disseminators

Many missionaries want to do more than spread the word; they want to spread the plants, too. Panayoti and Gwen Kelaidis have discovered many species and subspecies on hunts through the Rockies. They collect a few seeds and grow the plants in their home garden. Some of the results are taken to their friend Kelly Grummons, who propagates them for a retail nursery in Denver, Colorado, where they go from discovery to the public in just a couple of years.

Grummons's mission is to enlarge the nursery repertoire from the same old dozen or so plants, and also to make available to people in his area a remarkable variety of herbaceous plants that they, too, can grow. In the late 1980s, Grummons joined the staff of an old family-owned retail nursery called Paulino Gardens. The selection of perennials, arranged alphabetically, was then about 10 feet deep and 20 feet long. Now it is over 200 feet long and the plants are plucked up nearly as fast as they're set in the rows.

Because of his great success, Paulino Gardens supports whatever project Grummons wants to undertake. He has an unparalleled freedom to propagate any plant, and he has now transformed the nursery business in Denver. When he found a unique *Dianthus* among the potted plants, for example, one with black stems unlike its green-stemmed brethren, he propagated it vegetatively to add a new plant to the selection. He produced sal-

able plants in one-gallon containers in a year and named his introduction 'Dark Eyes'—a collector-missionary's dream.

Most retail nurseries are reluctant to take risks, afraid to invest in the untested or unfamiliar that the public may or may not buy, but as all good merchants understand, only innovation can make a business grow, and the most successful are those that offer unusual plants to push the limits of the market. As consumers, gardeners also have to be willing to communicate their desire to expand the range so purveyors will broaden offerings. This is, after all, how the containerized herbaceous-perennial movement revolutionized the retail nursery business over the last decade—in response to consumer demand.

Western Hills Nursery (pages 91–95) has been trading in futures for a quarter century. Not only has this West Coast retail nursery made unusual plants available to the public, it has inspired a generation of gardeners to be adventurous. They sell thousands of different plants in a place conceived by the nursery's late founders, Marshall Olbrich and Lester Hawkins—two esteemed collectors.

Pete Ray and Jean Emmons, who own Puget Garden Resources, have a new wholesale-only nursery. They would rather deal with plants than with the public, the rigors of retail, or deadlines of mail order. Exquisite gardens in the Seattle area—both humble and grand—owe much to these propagating pioneers. Among the plants they often carry are *Phygelius* 'African Queen' with pendulous scarlet flowers, a *Penstemon* 'Rich Ruby' with near-black flowers, a green and yellow variegated *Hydrangea macrophylla*, and *Dierama pulcheriamum* (angel's fishing rod or wand flower).

The plight of the Cyclamen, ABOVE, *spurred worldwide conservation efforts affecting the plants' habitats, harvesters, purveyors, and markets. All gardeners must do what they can to preserve plants. One way is to buy only nursery-propagated plants and grow them well, such as the yellow slipper orchid,* Cypripedium calceolus, OPPOSITE.

Conservators

Many missionaries are passionate conservationists who collect in order to preserve endangered plants. There are two types of conservation collectors, as well. All grow plants and grow them well. But while the passive gardeners shop, the activists *propagate*. Decades ago, no serious environmentalist would have lifted a plant from the wild, and the hands-off approach is still the best. But with habitats falling to development daily, even environmentalists have to intervene to rescue and to undertake conservation through propagation.

Tony Avent of Plant Delights Nursery, in Raleigh, North Carolina (pages 97–99), searches for native plants that have been overlooked as garden possibilities. With permission from local conservation agencies, he propagates endangered species such as the remarkable native *Baptisia arachnifera,* whose silver leaves look like a florist's eucalyptus.

Bill Brumback, Conservation Director for the New England Wildflower Society, tells the story of a lecture given at a symposium on North American terrestrial orchids in 1981. The optimistic speaker C. T. Riley said, "Imagine, for a moment, vast fields of orchids spreading out in all directions. Imagine a rainbow of reds and yellows, greens and whites. Now consider that I am not imagining Hawaii, Thailand, or Singapore, but Michigan, Ohio, or Illinois. I foresee a day," Riley went on, "when the volume of trade in orchid bulbs will rival that of the fancy tulips and hyacinths." Unfortunately, it hasn't come to pass. "Despite the laudable optimism," says Brumback, "there is no nursery engaged in large-scale commercial production of terrestrial orchids today."

Rare bulbs have been wild-collected in Turkey for over a century, primarily because Turkey has a more widely diverse native flora than does any European country, even North Africa. Located between the steppes of Central Asia and the moderate Mediterranean, the Eastern European woodland and the deserts to the southeast, Turkey's several habitat types offer a rich resource. In the late 1970s, concerned horticulturists and environmentalists realized that Turkey was on the verge of a conservation disaster. But although organizations such as the World Wildlife Fund, Natural Resources Defense Council, and the Flora and Fauna Preservation Society held meetings and published articles and proposed legislation, the bulb exporters balked. In 1987, TRAFFIC (Trade Records Analysis of Flora and Fauna in Commerce) published a paper on the case of *Cyclamen,* which at last began to have an impact.

The best solution for the trafficking problem is to have the same villagers who gathered the bulbs turn to their cultivation. In 1993, the first farm to produce bulbs commercially was founded in the tiny Turkish town of Dulmugöze. There, beneath groves of walnut and cherry trees, places unutilized by farmers, the bulbs are finally being grown.

Mail-order Nursery Fare

J. C. Raulston says, "Horticulture is a lifestyle, not a business." Avid collectors dream of having a successful specialty nursery growing favorite plants and shipping them to like-minded gardeners. The reality can be less than ideal, and those who are in the industry usually do it for love. The reality has more to do with power failures on 0-degree nights and frantic packing of boxes filled with orders to ship within the short period of favorable weather.

For gardeners, however, shopping by mail is the best way for them to acquire unusual plants.

FAR LEFT: Clematis *'Betty Corning' from Arthur H. Steffen, Inc.* CLOCKWISE FROM TOP LEFT: *The annual vine,* Mina lobata, *from Thompson & Morgan, has flowers that change color as they age—from red to cream; old-fashioned cup and saucer vine* (Cobaea scandens) *from J. L. Hudson, Seedsman; yellow pitcher plant* (Saracenia flava) *from California Carnivores; bizarre snail flower* (Vigna caracalla [Phaseolus caracalla]) *from Thompson & Morgan; Primula aucaulis 'Mark Viette', from Andre Viette Farm & Nursery; double oak-leaf* Hydrangea quercifolia *'Snowflake' from Heronswood Nursery.*

Not all the plants shown on these pages will be offered every year from the nursery cited: the stock varies. But the examples on these pages give a good idea of the incredible flora that can be found without leaving your armchair.

RIGHT, TOP TO BOTTOM: *One of the exquisite water plants available through the mail is the lotus—grand in bud, flower, and seed pod—* Nelumbo *'The Queen';* Xanthorhiza simplicissima, *from Forest Farm, is an interesting native sub-shrub that is easy to grow and not endangered but still extremely rare in gardens;* Campanula garanica *'Dickson's Gold' is the kind of plant that demand will bring to market.* OPPOSITE: *A temporary display of tender perennials (many from Glasshouse Works) in containers designed and planted by Nancy Goodwin and Doug Ruhren (pages 197-201) features a wide variety of* Coleus *cultivars and, peeking over the top, a variegated white and gray-green* Abutilon. *At the center of the arrangement is* Coleus *'Flirtin' Skirts', a brazen selection with burgundy-streaked green leaves edged with cream-colored frills.*

Mail-order Nurseries
includes
an annotated description
of the purveyors of extraordinary plants listed here,
followed by names and
addresses of places that,
from time to time, offer
most of the plants pictured
in this book.

FAR LEFT: *On some, too often*
rare, occasions, a plant's arrival
is a joy to behold. This Cornus
controversa *'Variegata'*
arrived exactly as shown from
Gossler Farm Nursery. LEFT,
TOP TO BOTTOM: Passiflora
vines like 'Ruby Glow' come
from Kartuz Greenhouses and
Logee's Greenhouses; Erigeron
pulchellus *'Meadow Muffin'*
from We-Du; Salvia van-
houtii *from Canyon Creek.*
RIGHT, TOP TO BOTTOM:
Scanning the catalogs can yield
bulbs, tubers, corms and other
geophytes for combinations such
as the one Robert Hays of the
Brooklyn Botanic Garden
created with non-hardy tuber
Canna *'Constitution' and*
tender grass Pennisetum
setaceum *'Rubrum';*
Magnolia *'Elizabeth' from*
Louisiana Nursery; a native
American plant that is being
rediscovered through the efforts
of collectors is the giant Rudbeckia maxima *with silvery-*
blue leaves from Prairie Nursery.

J. C. RAULSTON, SUPERSTAR

Dr. J. C. Raulston, Director of the North Carolina State University (NCSU) Arboretum, in Raleigh, has made a career out of curiosity. He is perhaps America's preeminent missionary: spreading the gardening gospel and disseminating plants. He is constantly experimenting with ones that are new to horticulture, whether discovered in foreign lands or in a drainage ditch down the street. Sometimes they are just new to Raleigh. Raulston's mission is to try out nearly any plant he thinks might be able to stand the muggy summers and cold, snowless winters in his climate and get the good ones to market.

If hoarding is the sin of the collector, then Raulston is an angel. *Generous* is an understatement. Botanical garden directors have complained that, although he has passed ten plants to them, only one or two have great potential. But Raulston's mission is to try enough new plants to discover which ones are truly spectacular, and among those, which ones will perform outstandingly in a given location. Once on a trip, he spoke with a garden curator who was having a plant pulled out because it sun-scorched badly. Raulston asked, "'Have you tried it in the shade?' They hadn't considered that," he recalls.

One of Raulston's favorite quotations is from Sir Peter Smithers, the noted Swiss plantsman, who said, "I consider every plant hardy until I have killed it myself." But the NCSU trials go well beyond a test of hardiness. Raulston believes in challenging the site and a plant to see what can happen. Several specimens of the same species or cultivar are often grown at NCSU. "A 60-foot-tall tree in the land-

Many plants with ornamental fruit for autumn and winter interest grow at the N.C.S.U. Arboretum, including hundreds of hollies, scores of noninvasive heavenly bamboos (such as Nandina domestica, OPPOSITE), *and* Akebia quinata (ABOVE), *an invasive grower that must be confined to a trellis.*

scape cannot tell you anything about the ability of that species to grow here," Raulston says. "A single tree is not statistically valid."

The arboretum focuses on woody plants, especially evergreens. There are approximately 350 genera represented and about 4,500 taxa. The *Ilex* (holly) collection has become one of the largest in the world, with over 200 varieties bearing masses of scarlet, orange, yellow, and red fruits in the fall and into winter. There are many other berry plants at the arboretum, such as *Callicarpa* (beauty berry), *Nandina* (heavenly bamboo), and *Actinidia* (hardy kiwi). Birds have no trouble finding this place on the outskirts of town.

His desire to spread the word takes him all around the country showing slides in lectures on what plants might be in the garden centers in five to ten years. At the arboretum, there is a rather unconventional attitude. People are not encouraged to steal plants, of course; but with permission, professional growers are urged to take cuttings of nearly anything, unless it has a sign saying that is still being observed, or it isn't a good candidate for mass production.

Raulston gathered some of the treasures in South Korea, but he also reminds us that in a given 5-mile radius from any place in the United States, there are new plants, seedling variants, and mutations that might be distinctive and worthy of introduction to gardens—if anyone chooses to see them. That fits perfectly with the stated purpose of the arboretum: "[to] collect, evaluate and encourage commercial production and use of a wider range of ornamental plants in the nursery/landscape industry."

SHE STOOPS TO CONQUER

Many collectors tell of a single moment that changed their lives. For Nancy Goodwin, a plantswoman from Hillsborough, North Carolina, it was a special day in a special place, when she saw a certain plant for the first time. "In 1963, on my second trip to England, we were having tea with friends in their garden and I looked down and there it was, one single cyclamen," she says. "I simply couldn't believe it was hardy. I can still see that plant." She came back to North Carolina with seed. "Something attracted me to them, I can't explain it. The foliage is so exceptional—every plant has different leaf markings." Goodwin tried to find more cyclamen to grow. She couldn't.

About 1977 the Cyclamen Society was formed in England, and she obtained seed to see if they could grow in her Zone 8 garden. Then Goodwin collected seed from the plants that she successfully grew. In 1983, she started Montrose Nursery to make these plants available to American gardeners. Goodwin was able to isolate seedlings and sell ones with white or pink flowers and silver foliage markings, or ones with solid pewter or bottle-green leaves.

These cyclamen, hardy by species from Zones 5 to 8, are members of the *Primulaceae* (primrose) family. *Cyclamen hederifolium* is the hardiest and easiest species to grow. It blooms from August to October as the leaves emerge. The beautiful leaves outshine the delicate pink or white flowers that are borne above the foliage on long, straight stems. Just as leaf colors vary, forms do as well, and may be heart shaped or lobed like English ivy (*Hedera helix*): hence, the species epithet.

Tubers develop the first year from sowing, and

OPPOSITE: *The* Cyclamen, *which leaf-out and bloom in the fall, bring a new season of gardening to the South.* ABOVE: *Each plant has markings on its leaves that last until spring.*

after five years, may be as large as grapefruits. Transplanting is best in the fall. They grow just beneath the soil surface, and tolerate dry shade—a boon to gardeners with that condition (just about everyone). As the flowers fade, their stems begin to corkscrew, bringing the ripening seed capsules close to the mother corm. Goodwin lets the seed ripen over the winter outdoors. They are fully ripe in May and June, but just before that, she gathers them to send to society seed exchanges and to sow for her collection.

Goodwin confirms that one of the stories cyclamen fans have told about the pitfalls of propagation is true: Ants do steal cyclamen seeds. "Every fall I would go out and count the plants and see if I had the same number as the year before. I always had more—they were naturalizing," she exclaimed. "But I noticed that new plants were growing in some strange places. Many were quite a distance from the parent plants and also uphill. I knew that rain couldn't be washing the seeds up; something else had to be at work in the garden. One year, when the nursery had really taken off, I collected the seed capsules just before they were ripe and open and brought them into the house. The next morning, every seed was gone! Ants had made a pass through the kitchen and stolen them right off the counter.

By the end of ten years in business, she offered thirty different species and selections, but closed the nursery in 1994 because she didn't have any time left to garden. But far from being defeated by the experience, she urges anyone with the desire to try a nursery. "Do it, you'll never regret it."

Retired biology teacher Dr. Frederick Case and his wife, Roberta,
live in a natural habitat garden in Saginaw, Michigan. They didn't set out to design an environmentally sound landscape; their creation is inspired by nature. It just makes sense.

"First and foremost," Dr. Case says, "we are wildflower gardeners." The Cases rehabilitated the rem-
nant of beech/oak forest surrounding the garden, and cleared a pond of weeds and debris. Their planted
spaces range from near wild to highly cultivated with everything in between, even lawn. Closest to the
house is a rock garden filled with alien and native plants in a meticulous order, but the areas along the
edges of the woods are developed for the Cases' most treasured collections—woodland, bog, and rock
plants—and are homes to countless North American wildflowers in impressive stands. Celandine poppy
(*Stylophorum diphyllum*) blooms in huge drifts; carnivorous plants of every imaginable type are here; and
then there are the trillium. The Cases probably have the largest collection of trillium in the world.

Trained as a botanist, Fred Case has written extensively on hardy terrestrial orchids, pitcher plants,
and even fungi, but the assembled *Trillium* species have become legendary among collectors. The Cases
are just two within a small group of people who are experimenting to help these plants find their way
into North American gardens, selecting sturdy specimens and ones with up-facing flowers, or those

OPPOSITE: *Dr. Fred and Roberta Case live in a natural habitat garden in Michigan with a collector's rock garden near the house.
Their main collection is of plants in the genus* Trillium. Trillium grandiflorum *is naturalized on the edge of the renovated
woodland,* ABOVE, *where trash/weed trees have been removed and the native kinds encouraged.*

that reproduce readily and bloom quicker from seed. Roberta Case also does her own hybridizing, creating improved varieties. The collection of *Trillium* seems even more impressive since the plants have to adapt to extremes typical of the continental climate just east of the prairie in USDA Zone 5. The zone map defines the minimum winter temperature—10 to 20 degrees F below 0 here—but says nothing of the highs. "One year, we hit 107 degrees F—the year our son was born," says Mrs. Case. "Recently we had twenty days over 90 in August."

Their plants come from seeds collected by botanists all over the trillium's temperate range, and they also travel extensively—mostly on safari, shooting plants with a camera. "We've been on plant expeditions to nearly every part of the United States," says Dr. Case, who while serving in the army lived in Alaska, where he found alpines like *Orchis rotundifolia* and *Dryas drummondii*, Franklin's lady's-slipper and butterworts. It is hard to imagine this unassuming couple scrambling over mountain cliffs, braving Arctic ice floes, or knee-deep in Everglade marshes, but they have done that and more. They have seen all but one of the thirty or so native trillium in the wild.

I came to this Michigan garden on a rainy day in May not knowing exactly what I would find. Dr. Case told me not to expect too much—theirs was not a formal estate, he warned. I left feeling that I had met two of the most enthusiastic and friendly experts in the horticultural world. I also came away with a beautiful pink-flowered *Lewisia* stuffed in my camera bag by Dr. Case and two *Arisaema* tubers from Mrs. Case wrapped up like a snack in my pocket to take on the plane. She grew them from seed and experimented with speeding up their life cycle with fluorescent lights and the kitchen refrigerator—just another project to fill her spare time.

The garden is naturalistic in style. A small stream, ABOVE LEFT, *is planted with mostly indigenous plants that would be found in such a place. The Cases started the spectacular native,* Dodecatheon meadia (shooting star), ABOVE RIGHT, *from seed.*

From the Case collection, CLOCKWISE FROM TOP LEFT: *A* Trillium flexipes *hybrid;* T. simile *hybrid with pointed petals;* T. catesbaei *has ruffled edges and fades to pink; green* T. recurvatum; *a* T. flexipes *form; recurved petals on* T. erectum f. 'Album'; *yellow* T. albidum; *ribbonlike deep pink petals of* T. pusillum; *strange* T. flexipes × erectum; *leaf-mottling of* T. discolor. BELOW: T. sulcatum 'Patrick' *has a blood-red flower.*

When Dan Hinkley started a wholesale nursery specializing in rare plants in Kingston, Washington, he discovered several things. One was that he couldn't sell his plants. "Five years ago, I would take what I thought were excellent plants to nurseries, and the owners would say that they couldn't sell anything the public didn't recognize," Hinkley says. One was the holly-leaf Itea (*Itea ilicifolia*) with glossy evergreen spiny leaves and dangling racemes up to 12 inches long covered with greenish white flowers. "We had perfect plants in flower in 2-gallon pots," he recalls. "I think we ended up throwing them on the burn pile—nobody would take them."

Around that time, Hinkley went on a pilgrimage. "J. C. Raulston of North Carolina State set me up a self-guided tour of southeastern nurseries specializing in unusual plants. Everyone I visited asked me if I was doing mail order. I hadn't thought of it. But it was their assumption that you have to do mail order to extend your market.

"In 1992, we did our first catalog. We sent out twenty packages; it's funny, I can still remember all those customers' names." He accidentally did the right thing at the right time, and today's 104-page beautifully printed catalog is evidence. So is his spectacular private garden and immaculate nursery. In just a few years, the new mail-order nursery, Heronswood, became the premier American outlet for unusual plants. "In 1993, we had 2,400 orders," he says, "and some of those were in the $1,500 to $2,000 range. Can you imagine all those boxes?"

Heronswood has become a primary source for the plants we read about in English garden books.

OPPOSITE: *A view of the perennial garden shows plants with rust-colored parts, such as* Euphorbia polychroma *'Pilosa Major', and the teddy-bear-like dried flower clusters of* Pyracantha atalantioïdes *'Gnome'.* ABOVE: *Featured vines include golden hop (*Humulus lupulus *'Aureus' with the silver* Eryngium giganteum [*called Miss Willmott's Ghost*]), LEFT; *blue potato vine (*Solanum crispum *'Glasnevin'), detail,* CENTER, *and* RIGHT. FOLLOWING PAGES: *Gold gleams from feathery* Sambucus racemosa *'Plumosa Aurea', thistle-like* Centaurea macrocephala, *and* Weigela *'Rubidor'.*

Hinkley and his friends make yearly treks to see what English gardeners, growers, and collectors such as Christopher Lloyd, Roy Lancaster, and Beth Chatto are trying out.

Being on the edge of the Pacific also has other advantages. New Zealanders make frequent visits to this part of the world where the climate is compatible, to see what breeders like Dan Heims in Portland, Oregon (pages 83–85), are cultivating and to leave behind some of their best, such as *Fuchsia procumbens,* a creeping species with "up-turned jewellike flowers of purple and gold, red stamens and blue pollen, then large pink fruits," as described in the Heronswood catalog.

The colorful gardens at Heronswood are often dominated by purple and near-blue from plants such as cultivars of *Allium, Veronica,* and *Nepeta.* A new garden is being developed behind the house, just off a wooden entertaining space partially covered by retractable duck awnings and a startling grapevine: *Vitis davidii,* from Roger Gossler of Gossler Farm (page 223). It has huge green leaves and amber twining stems covered with soft thorns.

The most mystical spot is the woodland garden beneath limbed-up Douglas firs. There, countless forest dwellers grow lush. The light shade and raised beds filled with fir bark and manure-enriched soil foster giants. A mat of the native ground covering dogwood, *Cornus canadensis,* is the largest I have seen. Heronswood's signature plant and a best-seller, *Corydalis flexuosa* 'Blue Panda', grows here, too.

Perhaps the most eerily bewitching botanicals are, however, the *Cardiocrinum giganteum* lilies, favorite of the late English garden marker Gertrude Jekyll, which grow in an incredible stand. Towers shoot-

ABOVE LEFT: *New areas of the garden are always being developed to showcase plants, such as an ornamental rhubarb* (Rheum palmatum *'Red Herald'). The amazing grape vine* (Vitis davidii), ABOVE RIGHT, *with huge leaves—up to a foot across—and soft rust-colored new growth and "thorns" came from Roger Gossler (page 223), and now climbs up the covered deck by the house.*

CLOCKWISE FROM TOP LEFT:
Filipendula ulmaria *'Aurea'*; *variegated shrub/tree,* Aralia elata *'Variegata'*; *Dan Hinkley's selection of the sycamore maple,* Acer pseudoplatanus *'Puget Pink', has incredible shrimp-colored new foliage; a wonderful blue-purple combination woven through with trailing* Petunia integrifolia *and the straight and tall variegated* Scrophularia aquatica *'Variegata'; fern,* Gymnocarpium dryopteris; *the side lawn garden is attractive for its many foliage textures from perennials, shrubs, and trees;* Astrantia major; *the perennial garden.*

ing 8 or more feet up to the sky bear huge white trumpets that fill the evening air with their heavy scent. These lilies may be offered in the catalog someday.

A listing of fifteen *Hypericum* is impressive, but pales in comparison to the *Hydrangea macrophylla* total of more than fifty cultivars. There are more than twenty *Clematis* species—not varieties—and remarkable *Codonopsis* species, shrubby vines with tiny bell-like flowers.

Another whimsical genus is *Dierama*, bulbous plants that send up fishing-rod stems that are more aptly described in the catalog as "evergreen grasslike foliage and dazzling arching canes of dangling flowers of soft pink marbled with darker shades."

It's hard to imagine, but the goal is to make the list more and more sophisticated. "I don't think you have to offer the same thing every year," says Hinkley, whose ambitions are boundless. It takes three months' work to put the catalog together. The task of organizing all of the aspects of the business got a little easier when Hinkley's partner, Robert Jones, left his job as an architect to come into the business full time. And Hinkley quit teaching horticulture in 1995. Hinkley has a gift—an ability to not only recognize spectacular plants, but to also propagate them. There are some people who just seem able to make anything grow, and this magician is one of them.

M I S S I O N A R I E S

OPPOSITE, CLOCKWISE FROM TOP LEFT: *Nine-foot-tall lilies in the woodland,* Cardiocrinum giganteum; *a section of the woodland walk with Japanese maple and* Corydalis spp.; *variegated columbine (*Aquilegia vulgaris *'Variegata') grows in the shadow of* Robinia pseudoacacia *'Frisia', and orange* Trollius chinensis *flowers light a woodland path; a blue border in the perennial garden.* ABOVE: *Plum colors highlight one area with the familiar barberry,* Berberis thunbergii *'Atropurpurea', fronted by* Rosa rubrifolia (R. glauca), *a hint of* Heuchera villosa *'Palace Purple', and a bluer froth of* Nepeta *flowers (catmint).*

Suddenly, "rose rustling" has become a horticultural household phrase. The practice of tracking down old varieties began very recently compared to rose cultivation, which has been going on for about 5,000 years.

Margaret Sharpe and Pam Puryear and a few other Texas gardeners were all fed up with modern finicky hybrid tea roses and intrigued by the old shrubs that grew in the yards, abandoned lots, and cemeteries in their area. While prowling around one old homestead in search of blooming plants to take cuttings from, they were greeted by an angry homeowner, shotgun in hand. The next time they went out, someone said, "Let's go out and rustle us some roses." The Texas Rose Rustlers were born.

Mike Shoup was in the wholesale plant business at the time. He, too, had an interest in the roses that throughout the decades have done very well on their own; when other roses burned to a crisp in the Texas summer heat or came down with every disease muggy air may foster, some old-fashioned shrubs would be thick with flower clusters. In the early 1980s, Shoup met Puryear and began propagating the Rustlers' discoveries and joining them on safari. As the stock grew, Shoup and Dr. William C. Welch of Texas A&M University started a mail-order catalog, *The Antique Rose Emporium,* which Shoup owns today.

79

The Antique Rose Emporium in Texas has become a destination for gardening tourists from Austin and Houston. OPPOSITE: *A bower of climbing roses clamber up posts and drape across ropes.* ABOVE: *Mike Shoup's goal is to show people how roses, especially tried-and-true old varieties, can be used in the landscape just as any other woody flowering ornamentals. The gardens are made in the styles of the buildings they surround, such as this Victorian house.*

In most cases he does not ship roses bare root, unlike nearly every other rose purveyor, and he does not graft them onto a rootstock of another rose. These are own-root plants. Shoup and many other gardeners believe that, though it might take longer to produce a plant without grafting, the result is a sturdier, healthier rose. The desired variety can also be much more hardy than its understock. Some gardeners suspect that modern roses are grafted onto roots as tender as USDA Zone 7. Even though the grafted rose is hardy to Zone 4, it may die at root level when the temperature hits 0 degrees F.

Shoup takes the interest in preserving old garden roses a few steps further. Concluding that these reliable plants do not have to be coddled in the rigid rows that have become the style in gardens of hybrid teas, he uses them in displays as landscape and garden plants: for the perennial border, foundation planting, or privacy hedge, for instance. For one area, he planted a huge hedge of white *Rosa rugosa* 'Sir Thomas Lipton' from 1900, as an impenetrable security barrier that blooms.

Shoup will eventually exhibit nearly all the possible uses of these roses. He moved an old building to show how they might have grown originally in a cottage-garden setting, and recently, a Victorian house was relocated to the property and a garden built around it in that period's more formal style.

His gardens nearby the attractive home he shares with his wife, Jean, in Brenham, Texas, are not really near anything else. Brenham, an old German settlement town, is approximately equal distance between Austin and Houston. Yet, at rose time in April, cars overflow the parking lot and line the road with people desperate to see and buy. With his collection of 250 varieties of old roses, Shoup has created an attraction that people drive miles to see.

Different styles of buildings from many periods have been brought to the site, and gardens are made to complement them. Some are humble old farm buildings, ABOVE LEFT; *others are grander, such as the Texas Victorian* (PRECEDING PAGE). *In all cases, as in the cottage garden planting,* ABOVE RIGHT, *roses meld with other flowers, such as the deep pink double opium poppies* (Papaver somniferum).

Dependable roses, CLOCKWISE FROM TOP LEFT: *'Fortune's Double Yellow', named for hunter Robert Fortune, who found it in China in the 1850s; 'Yvonne Rabier'; the modern climber 'Alchymist'; blowsy 'Marchioness of Londonderry'; 'Seven Sisters'; spreading, ever-blooming 'Perle d'Or'; tea-rose-like 'Maréchal Niel'; bright pink 'John Cabot'; 'Sombreuil'; striped 'Variegata Di Bologna'.* ABOVE: *Shoup named 'Katy Road Pink' for its discovery place.*

Dan Heims has a reputation for being the king of "variegation," but his hand-some Portland, Oregon, garden offers countless discoveries. Heims is a collector of the first order, and quite competitive in his craving. He says he collects traits. He gets an idea about what a plant might be in its ultimate form, finds variations with the characteristics he seeks, and then casts them onto the market like dandelion seed. He wants everyone to share his discoveries of sensational foliage.

He finds plants in several ways. Whenever he goes to a nursery he asks the owner, "Do you have any-thing odd or unusual?" He also has found that among the nursery rows of very regular plants, there is often one with a slightly different characteristic. Perhaps it is sturdier growth, bigger flowers, or maybe a hint of variegation. It doesn't always work, but most finds are substantially different from their progenitors.

On a recent trip to an Ohio nursery, he remarked to his companions that he had never seen a varie-gated sport or mutation of an alumroot, *Heuchera* 'Palace Purple', and then he turned around and there it was. Dan Heims calls this "sportfishing." The catch of that day is now called *H.* 'Patchwork'.

Another method is to start many seedlings and then hunt for unusual traits among the progeny.

OPPOSITE: *Members of Dan Heims's collection of* Heuchera, CLOCKWISE FROM TOP LEFT: H. sanguinea *'Silver Veil'*; H. *'Persian Carpet'*; H. sanguinea *'Firefly'*; H. *'Pewter Veil'. Heims's garden,* ABOVE, *looks traditional at first glance; but the plants that populate this place exhibit their guardian's fascination with variegated and colorful foliage. There are dozens of* Pulmonaria, Heuchera, Euphorbia, *and ferns, along with a remarkable variegated horseradish and rhubarb.*

For the last several years, Heims has concentrated on *Heuchera* (he has introduced twenty), *Pulmonaria* (lungwort), and is beginning to experiment with *Tiarella* (foamflower). Any plant with a desirable trait is grown in the garden for three years to test its habit and reliability. Then, the best get official names and go into micropropagation (page 219), whereby one plant can become 100,000 in a year.

According to guidelines from the organization whose own name is a mouthful, the International Commission for the Nomenclature of Cultivated Plants of the International Union of Biological Sciences, new plant names should be fancy. Heims claims to choose ones that describe the plant, but his idea of a description takes a bit of poetic license. One of his early selections was an unusual hosta with large sickle-shaped leaves. He wanted to call it 'Emerald Waterfall', but a British friend said that *Emerald* was too much of a mouthful.

Heims retorted with "Jade."

"All right, 'Jade Cascade'," said the Briton.

"Chills went up my spine," says Heims.

And you can see with the delight that he shows even in retelling the story the enthusiasm this man has for every discovery, invention, selection, and epithet. To him, *Hosta* 'Jade Cascade' tells a buyer exactly what he or she will get, as do names like *Heuchera* 'Pewter Veil', *H.* 'Chocolate Ruffles', or *H.* 'Persian Carpet'.

His new pulmonarias were selected for large flowers, usually blue, that stand up above the foliage. Some have pure platinum-white leaves, or silver spots, speckles, or splashes. Another feature of his creations is that any plant that exhibits even a hint of mildew (inherent in *Pulmonaria*) gets "hoicked" out of the soil and thrown away. His are disease-resistant plants with startling foliage color, and, though you can't always tell what you'll get from a name, you can make an educated guess that when you see a pulmonaria called 'Spilled Milk', it's one of Heims's varieties.

ABOVE LEFT: *The view from the house takes in a colorful banana* Ensete maurelli. ABOVE RIGHT: *White variegated* Scrophularia aquatica *'Variegata',* Lonicera nitida *'Baggesen's Gold' under a golden* Robinia pseudoacacia *'Frisia' tree.*

Some of Heims's Pulmonaria *discoveries and favorites,* CLOCKWISE FROM TOP LEFT: *P. 'Spilled Milk'; P. 'Roy Davidson'; P. 'Berries and Cream'; P. 'Leopard'; unnamed selected seedling; P. longifolia 'E. Bertram Anderson'; popular parent P. 'Margery Fish'; P. 'Little Star'; P. 'Purple Haze'; unnamed seedling.* BELOW: *P. rubra 'Redstart' is a large-leaved cultivar Heims uses in his breeding programs.*

What do you get in over a half century of collaborative gardening and collecting? The story of passionate rock gardeners Geoffrey Charlesworth and Norman Singer, and a whole lot of plants.

In his book, *A Gardener Obsessed* (1994), Charlesworth writes about the different kinds of zealous gardeners. First are the *activators*—the organizers of clubs, for instance. *Contemplative gardeners* are nature lovers with "benches in their gardens they actually sit on." *Cerebral people* look at a garden as a laboratory or a museum. *Arcane types* understand hybridizing or pruning techniques, for example. *Artists,* he says, plan a garden first. *Technicians* build walls and stake their delphiniums so you know they will survive the next hurricane. Charlesworth and Norman Singer have a bit of all these attributes, but are mostly *seedlovers.* These are unquestionably the most obsessed and probably the most important contributors of new plants to our gardens.

Charlesworth and Singer propagate 4,000 plants from seed each year—not 4,000 individual seedlings, but 4,000 species to sow and grow. Every year, they each make seed orders and there often is overlap, but in the end, about 3,000 different plants are started. Anything they have read about and not seen, seen and not grown, or merely never heard of are bought or traded for from the dozen or so societies to which they belong. They are missionaries because they spread the word about rock-garden plants, and disseminators because they start so many plants from seed. For years, they held a Labor Day sale to share extras; the proceeds go to the North American Rock Garden Society (NARGS).

In 1971, the two men—who met in England during World War II when Singer was stationed in

87

OPPOSITE: *The wild garden with a blue* Aquilegia *sent as seed from Scottish friends, yellow* Cypripedium calceolus, *red* Primula japonica, *and the large leaves of* Petasites japonicus. ABOVE LEFT: *The scene from the edge of the woodland.* ABOVE RIGHT: *The view toward the barn of the long border of dwarf and mid-sized conifers in every imaginable color.*

Charlesworth's homeland—bought land in Massachusetts as a weekend house. They retired there in 1981 to garden full time. As if starting so many plants and developing old farmland into rock and woodland gardens over several acres were not enough to occupy them, they both write on the subject of rock gardening.

But Singer's waking days have also been occupied by his deep involvement in NARGS. The society is one of the most prestigious in the world. (Singer and Charlesworth have both received the NARGS Award of Merit.) From 1992 to 1994, Singer served as the organization's president. He has worked tirelessly to promote rock gardening, and has influenced collectors in this book. (Panayoti Kelaidis, for example [pages 161–63], credits Singer with inspiring his own career.)

Their gardens are many—beds everywhere. As competitive plantsmen, they agreed that in order to avoid confrontation they would adopt a strict policy of separate beds. Several are designed and inten- sively planted areas with collections of conifers, and there are woodland and bog plantings, too, but the cultivation of alpines is central to the landscape. These low, rock-hugging miniatures fill island beds varying in size from about 10 by 20 feet to one that is the size of a house. One of the earliest gardens was made in what must have been the foundation of a barn or a stable.

The men plant in the existing soil that ranges from acid sand to rubble. Here and there, they dig pockets and install the appropriate medium before placing a seedling in its home. Some are made of pure sand. And a few areas were carved out of compost heaps, so the range is great.

"When we started, we used to cover every bed with Christmas tree boughs, but it's too much trou- ble," says Charlesworth. "If a plant can't make it here, then we don't need to grow it."

ABOVE: *A section of an older plantings is a rock gardener's dream with tidy conifers and tiny herbaceous alpines.* OPPOSITE, CLOCKWISE FROM TOP LEFT: *The feathery seedheads of* Pulsatilla vulgaris *ssp.* grandis fimbriata *near the barn; the rock and gravel scree behind the house; alpines in pots on the deck; an amazing spring occurrence—*Campanula thyrsoides.

Many people say they owe their interest and success in gardening to a parent or grandparent or friend. It is unusual to find a great number of people who would all say they owe it to a nursery, but that's the case for many Northern Californians. "I'd never seen this genus before I went to Western Hills—now I collect every species I can find," is the familiar refrain; or "I saw this combination at Western Hills"; or "a trip to Western Hills changed my life." Gardeners in other parts of the country also credit Western Hills with inspiration and exposure to new plants. That has always been the goal of the nursery: to find, propagate, and pass along rare plants that are beautiful.

The names of the nursery's late founders are evoked in appreciation just as often: "I got that from Lester Hawkins," or "Marshall Olbrich traded me something for that." "They were Renaissance men more than gardeners," says Maggie Wych, an English-born former jewelry maker who inherited Western Hills when Olbrich died in 1991. "Lester was an economist and Marshall a philosopher. They loved art and music; they were broad, multifaceted men."

The two men left their San Francisco apartment in 1959 and moved to a 3-acre parcel, which is pretty much a canyon in Occidental, California, intending to build an old organic homestead. They began with an orchard and vegetable garden, but Hawkins was inspired by the "congested but magi-

Western Hills Nursery has become a necessary destination for all gardeners on the West Coast and all who visit Northern California. The path along the hillside that leads to the house affords a trip through a living catalog of must-have plants for garden-ers—especially from warmer climes where the Agave americana *can send up its remarkable flower spike,* OPPOSITE.

cal" plantings made by Eric Walther at Strybing Arboretum in San Francisco, and set about clearing away the blackberries and poison oak and moving earth to build a "paradise garden." He filled in low areas, scooped out others and created several raised berms. He also developed narrow furrows to direct the water as it runs down the steep sides of the land and into what is now a pond. The little runnels weave down the hillsides from the road on one side of the property and from the steep slopes on the other sides.

The garden is truly made of rooms, each a whole new place with a tone and temperament all its own. And plants! Turn one corner and you'll find a remarkable barberry like none you've ever seen, but then a few paces more, and another outdoes your former favorite, and so on. These include evergreens: *Berberis jamesiana,* with little dangling coral berries; *B. darwinii* and *B. linearifolia* 'Orange King' have orange-sherbet-colored flowers.

Wych's tour through the garden includes some of the highlights from the last twenty or so years. "A *Cornus controversa* 'Variegata' (variegated pagoda dogwood) was one of Marshall's pride and joys, and then there's a *Rhododendron* cross I believe he grew from seed. I think one of the parents was the native *R. occidentale,*" she says. "Have you ever seen a contorted camellia? There's one over here; I'm not sure I like it."

Euphorbia dulcis 'Chameleon' is a startling new addition to the dozen-plus species and cultivars of this genus of hardy and half-hardy plants. There are also countless penstemons, salvias, and geraniums.

ABOVE: *Paths wind across rustic bridges over ponds and streams.* OPPOSITE, CLOCKWISE FROM TOP LEFT: *The view of the gardens and nursery from the house; another path, under an* Aesculus pavia, *leads to a white* Clematis montana; *the three-story-tall Lady Banks's rose; spiky* Echium spp. *lean into the path (Lady Banks's rose can be seen lighted by sun in the distance).*

Hellebores are becoming very popular and new ones are being selected and propagated to extend the offerings. Seeds are also being sent from New Zealand, and many of the resulting plants will be for sale after observation in the garden.

Sales tables overflow with unusual varieties of familiar plants, such as a wonderful red-stemmed and bronze-leafed viburnum with harmonizing rose-colored buds and buff-pink flowers. "It may be one of the *Viburnum sargentii* cultivars—J. C. Raulston (page 63) wasn't sure either," says Wych. "Isn't it hot potatoes?"

Both Olbrich and Hawkins collected feverishly—always looking for something unusual. Wych remembers Hawkins as the gardener and Olbrich, the plantsman who "couldn't wait to get the mail to find an envelope of seed." But Hawkins had a strong interest in Australian and South African plants and loved to travel.

After Hawkins's death in 1984, Olbrich went on and in a way came into his own in the ensuing years. And the garden didn't fail, although it was harder to keep up. Wych came to the garden as a "water woman," just to lend a hand. She had moved from Northern England to a little cabin nearby. "I would come up here every morning and just loved it," she recalls. When Hawkins became ill, Olbrich asked her to come on full time. Then, in 1991, when Olbrich died suddenly of a heart attack, the gardens became hers.

The place has never looked better. It has taken several years, but Wych and the crew have brought them up to the status they enjoyed in the best of times, and now they are developing new garden spaces. She is also moving to improve propagation techniques and would like to increase the nursery volume. The reputation of the nursery has never faltered, and people from around the country, and even the world, still make yearly pilgrimages to the site. When Beth Chatto visited from England the year Hawkins died, she told him, "The plants have been good to you." And they had.

OPPOSITE: *Layers of light from the dogwood,* Cornus controversa *'Variegata'.* ABOVE LEFT: *This is a plantsman's garden where selections were made for foliage texture and color—as in the case of* Carex buchananii *with metallic-brown blades.* ABOVE RIGHT: *There are flowers here (*Rhododendron*), but the splashed white elderberry (*Sambucus nigra *'Pulverulenta') foliage color lasts for months.*

Tony Avent may be among the most determined and serious nurserymen ever to start a mail-order nursery—he certainly is the funniest one to ever write a catalog. The comprehensive descriptions of offerings from Plant Delights nursery, which he founded with his wife, Michelle, in the early 1990s, are a howl. Even the cover bears a red label stating, "Warning: The Horticulture General has determined that opening this catalog may cause loss of mental and fiscal control."

The introduction inside continues in a similar vein. "We support a bill to make kudzu our national plant. Besides, what else smells sweet, tries to take over when you aren't looking, sneaks around through cracks and crevices, and does a wonderful job covering its mistakes? No other plant more closely resembles our federal government!" And Plant Delights Nursery makes no secret of its goal: to "offer the best, the newest, and the strangest in perennials. Our specialty is hostas—you know, 'I've got both, the green and the variegated one.' We currently offer two hundred."

Avent's humor spreads over to the naming of plants. Disgusted by names like 'Gossamer Sunlight', this rebel has named his introductions *Hosta* 'Bubba', *Hosta* 'Elvis Lives', *Hosta* 'Elephant Burger'. The prices vary, but the catalog reminds, "There is no maximum order."

97

MISSIONARIES

Plant Delights Nursery offers many new and unusual plants. OPPOSITE: *A sterile, and therefore everblooming, "hardy" lantana (Lantana camara 'Miss Huff') may be able to stand temperatures of 15 degrees F or lower. This plant, discovered by Goodness Grows Nursery in Georgia, lives by the entrance to Tony and Michelle Avent's display garden,* ABOVE, *shown in its third year.*

In person, Avent is thoughtful and soft-spoken—not at all the cutup his catalog leads one to expect. Of course, he has a good sense of humor, but the jokes are a marketing strategy; since he cannot afford to put out a color catalog, Avent gives customers another attention-grabbing reason to hold on to it and order through the year.

After fifteen years as landscape director for the North Carolina State Fair, Avent retired in 1993 to devote himself full time to the nursery. He has very clear goals and a kind of business-school sense in addition to his humor. One story seems to tell it all. While breeding hostas, Avent came across one rather homely plant that did have a tiny bit of frosting in the narrow upright leaves that looked a bit like an infestaton of red spider mite. Avent knew that this plant's parentage and the pale dusting might make it a good one for collectors to have for breeding. Besides, he didn't know what else to do with it. He named the plant *Hosta* 'Out House Delight' and charged $200 apiece. He sold forty the first year he offered it. "Collectors will buy anything," he says. But truthfully, the progeny he has produced with this mangy parent are striking. He intuitively knew that there was promise in this "ugly plant with good genes."

For plantaholics, the most thoughtful thing about the catalog is the two-box system for checking off the ones you want to buy. "The first box is for the plants you plan to order on your first trip through the catalog," it reads. "Once you get to the end and realize that you have blown your budget, go back to the beginning, and using the right hand column of boxes, recheck only those items that you absolutely, positively can't live without! Simple enough. Have a great time!"

A tour through the young garden, ABOVE, *affords an opportunity to see plants chosen for foliage color and texture.* OPPOSITE, CLOCKWISE FROM TOP LEFT: *The wonderful blue stems of the American native,* Andropogon ternarius; *a planting with one of the golden false cypresses offered in the catalog* (Chamaecyparis pisifera *'Filifera Aurea Nana'*), *asters, and a silvery ground cover,* Stemodia tomentosa; Polygonum cuspidatum *'Crimson Beauty'; the future . . .* Hosta *'Uzo No Mai' (little turban).*

*Henry Francis duPont created the
gardens at Winterthur in
Delaware—famous for one genus,*
Rhododendron, *exemplified by
naturalized azaleas,* OPPOSITE.
*Plants with unusual flowers, such
as the hellebores, are popular with
specialists. The flowers of*
Helleborus orientalis, LEFT,
*are very variable among individu-
als, and petal colors change and
last for months. Another specialty
is the genus* Geranium. *The
hybrid G.* × *'Johnson's Blue',*
ABOVE, *is an example.*

Specialists

The narrower the focus of a collection, the wackier that the passion and the
person appear to an outsider. But to insiders, these hard-core enthusiasts
attain an even greater stature because those of us who are similarly obsessed
can appreciate the sophisticated scrutiny and concentrated analysis these

collectors express. Specialists seem instinctively to group plants into categories based on the way
they look, how they are related, the countries they come from, or the habitats in which they reside.
I call these specialists—taxonomy, morphology, and habitat collectors.

A taxonomy collector might gather all plants of one family, genus, or even species. A morphology collector gathers plants that have certain physical characteristics. A habitat collector has a particular environment in mind for a garden—woodland, desert, bog, prairie—or the site, itself,
dictates the plants that will be chosen. Some might be attracted to trees with needles for leaves.
Others seek ones with succulent foliage, or simply all plants whose flower color is white.

The Taxonomy Collector

Taxonomy is the study of the principles of classification. In botany, taxonomists are the people who keep track of the scientific standing and names of plants. The taxonomy collectors concentrate on one family or genus as the focus of the passion. There is a history of genera collection. In the United States, the duPonts specialized in azaleas and plants that share their habitat in such gardens in the Delaware Valley as Winterthur. Lionel Nathan de Rothschild created the famous Exbury Gardens in England to breed rhododendron and azalea hybrids.

If a person collects a family, say the grasses *Gramineae*, as does Rick Darke of Landenberg, Pennsylvania (pages 137–39), then all the grass plants are included in his passion. This is a large family of about 700 genera, including corn, wheat, and sugarcane, and 7,000 species, not including cultivars.

Judith Jones of Seattle, Washington, loves ferns—all kinds of tender and hardy ones that she sells through Fancy Fronds mail-order nursery. Jones is much sought after as a lecturer and pteriphile. She is not satisfied to offer more ferns than nearly anyone; she is selecting and hybridizing to make new ones. She is also plugged into the plant-hunter's network and often receives rare spores of plants from Japan (via John Mickel of the New York Botanical Garden), from expeditions to Chile (Berkeley Botanical Garden), from the former Czechoslovakia, and from Germany, and as she is especially pleased to note, from Michael Garrett, a commercial fern grower in Tasmania, who "sends me lovely heaps of sifted spores from down under."

There are retail nurseries dotted around the country that specialize in one genus or another.

Judith Jones specializes in ferns, ABOVE LEFT, *and sells them through her nursery, Fancy Fronds. The Watt garden in Armonk, New York,* ABOVE, *was an inspiration to hundreds of daylily enthusiasts.* OPPOSITE, ABOVE: *There are a few collectors who narrow their specialty to just the variants of one species, such as Iris sibirica. I. s. 'Summer Sky' is an example.* BELOW: *Kurt Tramposh's specialty wholesale nursery looks like a sea of hostas under high-limbed pine and oak trees.*

Robin Parer's nursery, Geraniaceae, north of San Francisco, is open by appointment only. She specializes in hardy geraniums and their close relatives, currently boasting 250 species and cultivars. Randy Harelson founded a very unusual specialty store when he moved to western Florida in the mid-1990s. The Gourd Garden is designed to look like a roadside gift shop of the 1940s. He features everything to do with ornamental gourds: seeds, plants, fruit, musical instruments, vases, birdhouses. If you can conceive of it, he has it.

A few taxonomy collectors narrow their acquisitions to a single species, but that doesn't always limit the variety. A plant such as *Iris sibirica* (Siberian iris) has hundreds of cultivars in an incredible range of colors from claret-red to near-black to sky-blue.

More collectors tend to confine their interest to a larger division: the genus. You might imagine that if there was only one genus at the center of a collection, that, too, could be restrictive, but consider how many kinds of *Rhododendron,* or *Rosa,* there are—species, cultivars, and hybrids—these collections could have thousands of individuals. In the genus *Hemerocallis* (daylily), for instance, there are some 35,000 named varieties.

Sydney Eddison (pages 133–35), in central Connecticut, collects daylilies. She was inspired by a visit to a garden in Armonk, New York, on Daylily Day. Paul and Louise Watt, illustrious members of the American Hemerocallis Society, had a large garden filled with a thousand daylily cultivars. Enormous, undulating beds ran around the large property like a river—surrounding an island of lawn

and house. It was overwhelming to any daylily gardener, but to society members who visited, it was a living catalog of the latest introductions and how they compared with their progenitors. It was a dazzling site on those days in mid-July.

Hosta collection often goes along with daylily devotion, and the collectors' ardor of each runs deep. Kurt Tramposh's wholesale nursery in Massachusetts is an astonishing sight, with acres of different hostas growing in a sea of green under high-limbed pine and oak trees. Several great *Hosta* collectors live in Ohio, such as Van Wade and Pete Ruh. *Hosta* fanciers seem to be everywhere, except Northern California—the voracious snail's dominion.

Other collectors may have more modest interests, but ones that fascinate nonetheless. David Culp, of Sunny Border wholesale nursery in Connecticut, has a collection of hellebores in his home garden that is becoming well known as these plants increase in popularity. They have wonderful foliage and flowers in partial shade; many are evergreen or semievergreen, and easy to grow. Perhaps most alluring is their blooming season—winter to early spring.

Brent Heath's family has been in the daffodil busi-

ness for three generations. During the Depression, the economy of Gloucester County, Virginia, was vitalized by a market in poor man's roses, as cut daffodils were sometimes called. The flowers were harvested as they opened, then boxed and shipped up the river to New York City.

Times change, but the Heaths' devotion persists to this single genus with thousands of cultivars. Only today, the bulbs are sold and the Heaths are most interested in creating new varieties along with preserving the oldest ones—many of which were lost except in the former farm fields.

Brent and Becky Heath of the Daffodil Mart are devoted to the genus Narcissus—*even their license plate,* ABOVE LEFT, *makes this clear. Many old species and varieties have grown for decades beside the riverbank,* ABOVE, *on the Virginia farm.*

The Morphology Collector

There are collectors like Brent Heath who devote themselves to a specific genus of bulbous plant. Others, like John Gwynne, collect one kind of plant that grows from a tuber: *Arisaema.* Still others may seek all *geophytic* plants, ones that grow from underground bulbs or tubers. Some collectors may be keen on flowering herbaceous perennials for their gardens, or concentrate on woody plants—trees and shrubs. Others might make gardens filled with plants that flower in only one color or have variegated leaves. All of these are examples of collections based on structure and form.

The branch of biology that deals with the physical aspects—the structure and form—of plants and animals is called morphology. Morphology collections can be quite general, and the themes may be clear only to the collector, because a wider variety of plants are allowed than would be in a taxonomy collector's patch.

Tom Krenitsky, for example, grows dwarf evergreens, a morphological specialty of many collectors. Krenitsky's North Carolina assemblage of dwarf evergreens is a garden first and a collection second. Before he arranged his shrubs, he brought in a landscape architect to lay out the planting. Now, not only does his garden boast some of the best specimens of mature, slow-growing conifers in any private garden, but they all support and reinforce the garden's structure. The imposed design allows him to grow many unusual species and cultivars with no danger of a hodgepodge look.

Jim and Conni Cross (pages 149–51) of Long Island, New York, also have a garden with many woody plants—Jim's special love. In this place, the design does not come from an imposed structure, but structure comes from the arranged woody plants that anchor and punctuate Conni Cross's exuberant color plays of annuals and perennials.

Garden designer Daune Peckham collects herbaceous perennials to test color combinations in raised beds in her garden in Little Compton, Rhode Island. She is attracted to flowers and their colors and uses them to make miniature paintings that she then interprets for her clients.

Many collectors crave the morphological aberration of variegation. Henry Ross in Ohio has a large collection of *variegates*—what plants with variegated foliage are sometimes called. Ken Frieling and Tom Winn find

Morphology collector Tom Krenitsky's passion is for dwarf evergreens, which he grows in a beautiful garden in North Carolina, BELOW LEFT. *Each selection is distinctive in shape and color,* BELOW CENTER, *such as* white Pinus densiflora 'Oculus-draconis', Cryptomeria japonica 'Globosa Nana', *and gold* Chamaecyparis obtusa 'Nana Lutea'. *Daune Peckham collects herbaceous perennials to test their colors in combinations,* BELOW RIGHT. *It is a movable feast of herbaceous plants in raised beds that she constantly fine-tunes, adjusting arrangements.*

105

that they are adding more and more variegates to their garden, also in Ohio, and to their catalog, Glasshouse Works (page 225). Richard Schock boasts more than a thousand variegated plants in his North Carolina garden.

Barry Yinger, the modern-day plant explorer (page 25), confirms that collecting variegated plants is a developing trend. He also notes that there is a growing passion among Americans for cacti and succulents. That is not news to Ruth Bancroft (pages 141–47), who has collected plants that store water in their stems and leaves for years. These flower too, often with huge colorful blossoms that may last only a day. The golden spines, silver threads, and dustings of diamonds on the leaves and stems of succulents and cacti in her California garden are nearly year-round attractions.

Marion Haffenreffer collects rhododendrons, ABOVE LEFT. She also specializes in understory plants, native wildflowers, and their analogous counterparts for a New England woodland habitat. Susanne Jett designed a garden for the Santa Monica, California climate, ABOVE RIGHT, with species that like hot, dry days and cool, misty nights. Beneath an olive tree grow a specimen New Zealand flax and green and gray Santolina spp.

The Habitat Collector

Tom Chakas of Berkeley, California, has about seventy species of the genus *Lavandula* (lavender) on his hillside garden. He is a taxonomy collector, but his garden is not made of just these plants. He has gathered many others that like the steep hillside, fast drainage, and moderate weather of his garden. It is a Mediterranean-style garden—the habitat sets the tenor of the collection.

Susanne Jett is a habitat collector, too. She grows plants from the Mediterranean basin and from regions with the same conditions. As a professional designer, she uses low-maintenance, low-water-use plants from the habitat that is very similar to the one in which she works: Los Angeles.

Habitat collectors often are stimulated by the place where their gardens reside, but some have an almost instinctual love for a certain kind of environment. Rick Darke (pages 137–39) credits a woodland spot where he grew up in New Jersey with inspiring his career. Many of the plants he loved as a boy wandering through Garfield Park grow in his Pennsylvania garden today. Judy Glattstein (pages 165–67) also bonds with the woodland and chose it as the theme for her garden and collections.

Marion Haffenreffer's Massachusetts garden receives nearly 50 inches of rain each year. This is a woodland, and that has directed her collecting. Her passion is hybrid rhododendrons, for which her garden is quite well known. She also has a sophisticated woodland understory garden with native and analogous wildflowers that she propagates. In another, wetter area, she grows *Primula* species, *Clethra alnifolia* (summer sweet), *Caltha pulustris* (marsh marigold), and other moisture-loving, shade-tolerant plants.

Sometimes a general habitat can narrow the focus of a collection. Several collectors, including Stan Farwig from Concord, California, and Sean Hogan, formerly of the University of California Botanical Garden at Berkeley, collect South African bulbs. These plants are unfamiliar to most of us, except perhaps for the Christmas amaryllis. But there are many genera—*Crocosmia, Tigridia, Freesia, Babiana, Ixia, Watsonia*—that are becoming more and more popular with gardeners in arid, warm-temperate climates.

South African bulbs, such as Lachenalia aloïdes *'Aurea',* BELOW LEFT, *are getting attention from specialists. Tom Chakas specializes in* Lavandula *in his garden, "Mediterranean Hillside,"* BELOW RIGHT. *He has seventy-five varieties.*

Lee Raden (pages 157–59) was so inspired by visits to alpine habitats that he designed an entire garden to imitate them. If you can identify with his feeling for his garden, then you can taste a bit of what the specialist collectors have: They can visit worlds away just by going outside their door. All this in the space of a single yard, and all because of the power of plants.

DENIZENS OF THE DARK

Arisaema species and other hardy aroids are the collector's collectible. These, and related members of the family *Araceae*, are perpetual love/hate plants—some people are fasinated by them; others find them disgusting. Commonly called aroids, they include many familiar plants, from *Philodendron* to *Anthurium, Zantedeschia* (calla lily), and *Spathiphyllum*. The ones we know best are tropical, but there are many hardy relatives that are wonderful for temperate-zone gardens, providing the gardener is a curiosity seeker who likes the hooded spathe over the flowering spadix that typifies this group. Most of the hardy ones hail from woodland habitats, and have the typical eerie flower structures and broad arrow-shaped, waxy leaves.

The arums are tuberous oddities with leaves that can be striking. *Arum italicum* cultivars, from the Mediterranean region, can have leaves splashed or veined with silver that appear in fall and persist through the winter, even in snow. It is easy to miss the spring flowers but hard to ignore the fruiting spikes—clublike structures covered with orange or scarlet berries that ripen in late summer as the new leaves emerge.

Arum maculatum, a native of the British Isles, has green leaves often splashed with black or purple, but is known best for its showy floral structure, a pale green spathe bordered in purple, pink, or white, and a spadix variably maroon or cream—thus, one of its common names: lords-and-ladies. But there are literally hundreds of common names for this plant, among them: babe-in-the-cradle, bloody-man's-finger, parson-in-the-pulpit, adder's-tongue and Kitty-come-down-the-lane-jump-up-

The genus Arisaema *includes bizarre and beautiful woodlanders, such as* A. sikokianum, OPPOSITE. ABOVE: *Aroid* Pinellia pedatisecta.

and-kiss-me. The most common name, however, is cuckoopint, from the Anglo-Saxon words *cucu* for *lively* and *pintle* for *penis*.

In comparison, the familiar native, *Arisaema triphyllum* or jack-in-the-pulpit, has a name that seems tame. But this *Arisaema* and its relatives make the most intriguing and in most cases, easy-to-grow candidates for the shade collector's garden.

Arisaema is the largest woodland aroid genus, with about 150 species worldwide. Nonetheless, these plants are rarely offered for sale, although most are easy to grow from seed and cultivate. John Gwynne (pages 119–23) has 40 kinds in his Rhode Island garden.

The North American native *Arisaema triphyllum* occurs naturally in the eastern woods, where they are not threatened but their habitats are. Some taxonomists believe there is only one species, and others count as many as four—the debate goes on. I have observed quite a bit of variation in leaf and flower in natural populations, which could be environmental, but traits as clear as white ridges in some individuals' leaves and widely differing colors of spathe lead me to believe that there are at least distinct subspecies if not entirely separate species. Most of the variations seem to persist when the plants are grown from seed away from their original homesites; but some variations disappear.

When John Gwynne refers to a thick blotchy-stemmed *A. triphyllum* in his garden as "she," he is not making a sexist remark. *Arisaema triphyllum* changes its gender according to the previous year's growing conditions. Young plants, usually with one three-part leaf, are male. When the plant is mature, a healthy growing season will result in a female the following year. The females are larger than the males, so the large one was indeed capable of creating cobs with scarlet berries. (The flesh on the berries inhibits sprouting and must be washed away for successful germination.) Many *Arisaema* species also produce side tubers as a means of reproduction.

Mature plants have one or two attractive leaves, which are often palmately divided and mottled with silver or maroon. Judy Glattstein, of southern Connecticut (pages 165–67), points out that the leaves are arranged like a T, unlike the evenly spaced trillium leaves they resemble. The elegant *A. sikokianum* may have clearly defined central silver zones on the leaves, depending upon the individual. Purchase one with colorful foliage since green ones tend to stay green through their lives of twenty-five years or so. *A. sikokianum* also has a beautiful flower, or more precisely, spadix and spathe. (The flowers are too tiny to see.) The spathe attracts the attention of pollinators, often flies, and also may disseminate the vaguely or profoundly malodorous attractant. The spadix underneath looks like a little dollop of melted marshmallow and has been described as an upside-down porcelain pestle.

Arisaema flavum, an alpine, is sometimes called owlface for its flower. The deep-brown hood of *A. griffithii* nearly closes over the spadix, which has a very long, stringy appendage that can creep along the ground for a foot or more—perhaps to provide a runway for crawling pollinators. Unfortunately, it is a bit harder to grow than some.

A. ringens is among the showiest, in and out of flower, with large, variably dark or light green leaves on plants that grow singly or in big clumps up to 3 feet across. Of course, the flowers are the attraction. Hidden within the leaves are thick spathes with fleshy recurved edges.

Arisaema ringens *has about the largest flower of the genus. It is also quite easy to grow. As with most of the genus, it wants a typical humusy woodland soil that is neither too wet nor too dry. The large leaves make this a good candidate for shade.*

"Some people's *ringens* have green lips, but mine are always purple or black," John Gwynne says with a mischievous look in his eyes. Although they are generally regarded as plants that have to grow on you, Gwynne's glee over the Bela Lugosian creatures is infectious.

A. dracontium, green dragon, is the United States' other native species, growing in rich soil in woodland and stream sides in the Midwest, Quebec to Vermont, and south. The green spathe wraps around the spadix, which has a very long protuberance.

Mousetail, an *Arisaema* relative, properly known as *Arisarum proboscidideum*, might be the only one of this group that could actually be called cute. This aroid from the woods of Italy and Spain has a closed spathe with a little tail at the tip. *Pinellia* species are similar, but watch out: Some of these green-flowered plants, long used in Chinese medicine, can become invasive.

Most woodland types are happy with dappled shade, including up to a half day or more of sunlight if the planting medium is moist. If you obtain tubers, these can be planted in fall or spring, 3 or so inches deep. The roots emerge from the top, so enrich the soil above the tuber with bonemeal and/or manure. They can cope with dryness, and may even go dormant early in the season, or not come up one year at all. That doesn't mean they are dead—often they will be back the following year.

Bulb expert Judy Glattstein says that you can lift an *Arisaema triphyllum* in flower, take it to exhibit in a show, bring it home, and pop it back into the rich humus, and it will never even wilt. That practice can't be recommended, but these oddities are becoming more available from fresh seeds and dormant tubers, and should be adaptable additions to your botanical menagerie.

The "tails" that appear on some species either as extensions of the spadix or at the ends of the spathes may have evolved to help crawling insects get to the flowers for pollination. They may be a foot or more long. The Arisaema and their relatives are the most numerous aroids of the temperate regions. CLOCKWISE FROM TOP LEFT: Arisarum proboscideum (mousetail); Arisaema triphyllum; A. serratum; A. angustatum *var.* penunsulae *f.* variegata; Pinellia ternata; A. griffithii; A. dracontium; A. sikokianum.

CAN I GROW THIS PLANT?

Some of the plants shown here have never been discussed before in books or catalogs. To find out growing information ask questions. Where is this plant from? What is its native habitat like? What are the soil and moisture conditions? How warm and cold is the climate? What is the elevation? A plant from the seaside can withstand wind and maybe even salt spray, and it probably needs good drainage, because coastal soil is often sandy.

Corydalis flexuosa 'Blue Panda' is a plant that is gaining in popularity for its electric blue flowers that appear continually from spring to fall. But books have little cultural data on it, and even experts are guessing and experimenting. Research shows that this plant comes from the Baoxing and Wolong valleys in western Sichuan, where it grows on steep and shady slopes in moist, humus-rich soil. The approximate latitude is 30 degrees north (comparable to Jacksonville, Florida), but this area, close to the northeast corner of the Himalayas, is at elevations up to 10,000 feet. Even the valleys in this range could be quite cold in winter, and cool in summer. Dan Hinkley of Heronswood Nursery (pages 71–77) considers this to be a USDA Zone 5 plant. Good specimens grow in the Pacific Northwest with moderate moist winters and cool, dry, sunny summers.

Most plants can be pushed or pulled one zone. Many plants can be grown out of their range, if the spot is protected (see Nick Nickou, pages 39–41). I grow the vigorous climber, Lady Banks's rose (*Rosa banksiae*), against a protected corner of my house where an east-facing wall meets a south-facing one. This is a plant associated with Zone 8 gardens in England and South Carolina, where it scampers up buildings and even trees. The two-story tall plant blooms most years with thousands of flowers. The freak winter of 1994 severely knocked it back, but it survived to grow and bloom again.

When I had a roof garden where everything grew in containers, I selected plants from one zone colder since containers not only freeze down from the top as does the ground, but also in from the sides and up from the bottom. Because of wind exposure, the potted trees turned color two weeks earlier in the fall than the same ones on the streets below, and spring arrived two weeks later. Trying some special plants often means challenging nature. If the plants are not endangered, it is worth a try.

Don't be deterred if a plant is listed as being hardy to a warmer zone than yours. Denver's reliable snow cover keeps the ground from freezing, and excellent drainage often adds a zone of hardiness to herbaceous plants. I grow many tender plants and "winter them over" in a cold frame, if they are small, or in my unheated 40 degrees F mud room.

ABOVE: *The native bayberry* (Myrica pensylvanica) *grows along the beach in sandy soil; it is sun loving, wind tolerant, and resistant to salt. When a new-to-horticulture plant appears, such as* Corydalis flexuosa *'Blue Panda',* OPPOSITE, *everyone wants it. Discover its roots to learn its needs.*

Betsy Clebsch tells of the giant *Salvia dombeyi* that has grown to two stories high in its native Peru, although in her Northern California garden, it is a mere 3-foot-tall shrub. There are also species that nearly hug the ground (*S. argentea*), ones with cherry-red flowers (*S. greggii*), and others with blossoms as blue as the sky (*S. guaranitica* 'Argentina Skies'). And, of course, culinary sage, the common name for *Salvia*. Clebsch has more of these mint relatives than she can count, but doesn't consider herself a collector. "I don't have a salvia collection," she insists. "I have a garden."

It just happens to be populated with more than one hundred species and cultivars of a genus that now cohabit with roses, *Heuchera, Echium,* hardy *Geranium,* and others. She stresses the other plants in her garden because she sees the role of the salvias as being garden companion plants—part of the scheme. She will talk about a sage and its origins, culture, and habit, but just as quickly tell you which other plants look good with it. "Some people visit my garden and they never see anything but the salvias; just like rose lovers or fuchsia collectors," she says. "I've never been like that."

Salvias are distributed all over the world, except for Australia. Clebsch's climate is perfect for many of them. "Salvias are part of the native flora here as well," she says. Local salvias include chia (*S. columbariae*) and creeping salvia (*S. sonomensis*). Although she lives on the coast of Northern California, occasional fog does not influence the growing conditions as much as the sun and dryness. This arid climate

OPPOSITE: *The flower spike of* Echium pininana × wildprettii *shoots up through chameleonesque* Rosa mutabilis, *whose flowers deepen from pale apricot to deep pink.* ABOVE LEFT: *The garden in deer country is surrounded by a 5-foot-tall double fence.* ABOVE RIGHT: *Clebsch does not live by salvias alone—these plants like the company of silver artemisia and purple barberry.*

is very similar to that of the Mediterranean, and is loved by these plants. At least one Mediterranean-looking plant is from South Africa, though: *S. africana-lutea (S. aurea)*. It has a summer dormancy but blooms repeatedly with an especially big show in late winter to early spring. It is striking with russet-brown flowers protruding from pumpkin-orange calyxes, but it may be one of those esoteric specimens that collectors find weird but lovable, and others just find weird.

Clebsch's original garden on this property was several hundred yards down the hill, near the ocean. "It was a sheltered spot we found by accident—a strange and wonderful place where the Native Americans used to spend January and February," she says. The problem was the distance from the house. Nonetheless, she gardened there for fifteen years, driving the truck down and up the hill. But in winter, the truck couldn't make it through the mud and she had to walk. "I was in great shape then."

Her friend Gerda Isenberg, of the neighboring native plant nursery Yerba Buena, said, "Just move it up by the house where you can enjoy it." Clebsch started that day. She didn't exactly move the old garden (salvias do not like to be uprooted); she began a new one, shown here in its fourth year.

I thought that one of the reasons for the garden's relocation was for deer proofing, but it turns out that even the old garden was safely enclosed with a fence Clebsch swears by. "It's two fences, only 4 feet tall and separated by 4 to 5 feet. Deer won't jump over a fence unless they can see a clear place to land," she says. "I've never had any deer damage here." She has been planting the area between the fences, too, which used to be for wheelbarrow access, since, like nature itself, gardeners hate a vacuum.

With all her experience with salvias, this talented gardener still does not consider herself an expert. This is even more ironic because she is working on a book that will be the first devoted to the genus *Salvia*.

ABOVE LEFT: *Tall* Salvia karwinskii *matches the color of the masses of bright pink verbena.* ABOVE RIGHT: S. eigii *blooms next to the garden rake. Silver* Helichrysum splendidum *with yellow flowers complements the fragrant salvias.* OPPOSITE, CLOCKWISE FROM TOP LEFT: Salvia spathacea *with orange California poppy* (Eschscholzia californica); *woolly* S. argentea; *pink* S. recognita *in front of* Bulbinopsis bulbosa; *and* S. × 'Cienga de Oro'.

Hidden within a thicket of autumn olive, arrowwood, and blueberry is a small opening. Visitors have to crouch down a bit to pass through this carved-out breach in the bramble that leads to a winding tunnel of foliage. After a short, somewhat disorienting passage, a doorway of holly frames a cathedral of evergreen trees. It is a unique effect, and just a hint of the kind of inventiveness and design made by part-time gardener, artist, and full-time collector John Gwynne, on the shore of Rhode Island.

"Mine was a family of competitive gardeners," he says. "My mother's garden was on one side of the house, and my father's was on the other. I was the slave labor: hating weeding, hating gardening—bulldozers were fine, though." For his fifteenth birthday, Gwynne asked for a pond, and he still likes to move earth today, although without destroying the tenor of the setting.

As you walk within the natural thickets, you have almost no sense of where you are—no sense of where you've been or where you're going. This garden, more than most, is made of such distinctive rooms and experiences that the seemingly long walks from space to space actually take place in short distances. "My garden is too small for all the plants I want to grow, and too large to maintain," says Gwynne, who began

John Gwynne's main garden cannot be seen from the house or even from the property. The traditional entry garden is understated, ABOVE. To find the collector's garden, one must pass through a gash in the scrub and follow a winding path to a doorway, OPPO-SITE, that Gwynne formed in a holly hedge. There is his cathedral of Cryptomeria japonica 'Lobbii' trees with a boardwalk floor. Beyond this site is a lawn dusted in fallen crabapple petals with a celadon urn in the distance.

119

collecting with rhododendrons. "I first got hooked on rhododendrons, and friends would give me *layers* (stem cuttings rooted while still attached to the plant) of old ironclads, then I started getting into weirder ones; it grew to 500 kinds when I thought, 'This is crazy—all these colors, it isn't calm.' I decided, 'Okay, yellows here, reds here, pinks here—everything else gets tossed.'" Today most of his rhododendrons are in Edwardian biscuit colors, except in one place where he is carving a living sculpture.

"Because of space and the wind off the ocean, I couldn't do a real rhododendron woodland here, so I made a kind of punch bowl," he says. It is a large circle, about 30 feet across, open at one end to enter. The plants have been arranged for color and size and are pruned as well to go from ground level up to 10 feet. White flowering shrubs are at the axis and dark pinks at the opposite sides. Between them, the colors will blend together. "It's a garden for the twenty-first century," he says, looking to the time when the mature plants fulfill the design.

As the garden has grown, Gwynne seems to focus more on unusual plants; actually, on eerie, strange denizens of the woodland depths. He has become devoted to the family *Araceae* (page 111). In Britain, these plants are known by delightful names like cuckoo pints, lords-and-ladies, and mousetails.

"I've got one aroid, *Helicodiceros muscivorus,* a huge, really ugly Cretan—smells bad, too, terrible, invented by the devil," he says. The ones Gwynne treasures most, members of the genus *Arisaema,* have somber-colored hoods like cobras, and often an unpleasant fragrance. "Aren't they great?" Gwynne asks with delight, the consummate collector undeterred by a small matter like smell.

THE COLLECTOR'S GARDEN

PRECEDING PAGES, CLOCKWISE FROM TOP LEFT: *The lawn sprinkled with apple blossoms; the walk to the lawn passes by the* Rhododendron *"punch bowl"; a path at the rear of the garden features a framed view of the meadow beyond; the punch bowl garden will come into its own in the next century.* ABOVE LEFT: *A soft, biscuit-colored hybrid* Rhododendron *is a new collectible. The urn that forms the terminus of a major view,* ABOVE RIGHT, *is surrounded by plants with chartreuse foliage and backed by the magnificent dove tree* (Davidia involucrata).

Spectacular oddities of the Gwynne garden include, CLOCKWISE FROM TOP LEFT: Arisaema triphyllum *with pink and blue* Hyacinthoides hispanica (Scilla hispanica) *backed by cinnamon fern's* (Osmunda cinnamomea) *tan fertile fronds; bizarre flowers of* Arisaema griffithii; *leaves of* Astilboïdes tabularis *with the white flowers of* Allium ursinum; *species* Rhododendron sutchuenense *has new growth that makes the plant look somewhat like a pineapple; the tawny-golden bud of* Trillium cuneatum; *the orchid* Calanthe striata; *unfurling fronds of deer fern* (Blechnum spicant); *the mottled leaves of wild ginger,* Asarum arifolium.

To design a house around a plant collection sounds extreme, but that was the case with Diane and Jon Spieler's Lafayette, California, home, planned and executed to shelter not just them but their roses.

Because they live in deer country, the garden had to be protected. The architect, Jock McKay, created a U-shaped plan for the house; a wall forms an interior courtyard garden, designed by Jonathan Plant and Associates. The white stucco wall on the garden's east side affords complete protection for the roses. Portals were constructed in the wall to give visitors a peek inside as they walk to the front door. The white wall changes height and position so as not to be a relentless, visually unbroken barrier. But the first impression of the Spieler garden is not how beautiful it looks, but how incredible it smells, even from the winding driveway through the hills.

"I saw my first rose while visiting Buchart Gardens in Victoria, Canada," says Diane Spieler. "Of course, I had seen roses before, but I never really looked at them." She and Jon lived in a condo then, and they began collecting old-fashioned roses to grow in containers. As she became more dedicated, she began to specialize in antique roses: those bred before the introduction of the first hybrid tea rose, 'La France', in 1867. Today her collection includes species, antique roses, old garden roses, two of the

Within the walls of a new mission house, Jonathan Plant designed a deer-proof cloistered garden to house Diane Spieler's old-garden rose collection with a pool, OPPOSITE, *and gravel patio around a central fountain feature,* ABOVE.

China roses that were crossed with the European roses to create the first hybrid teas. She grows examples from the various historical classes of roses: *Rosa gallica,* and ancient forms of hybrids Alba, Damask, Bourbon, Portland, Centifolia, and Moss. She also has 'La France'.

No one is certain when roses first began to be cultivated (garden roses were found in Egyptian tombs), but fossils found in Colorado and Oregon show that this genus has been around for at least 32 million years. They are native to many parts of the temperate world and are favorites everywhere. The roses Shakespeare knew were probably ones like the dog rose, *Rosa canina,* or *R. eglanteria,* whose foliage when crushed smells exactly like green apples. In *Gerard's Herbal* of 1597, fourteen roses were mentioned. By 1800, after years of French breeding, there were a thousand. The antique roses bloom only once a year—although Spieler maintains that this one-time bloom is more worthwhile than the perpetuals that bloom about as much but are divided between the spring flush and late-summer rebloom.

She trims and deadheads blossoms diligently. "In the winter, I cut back most of the rose canes and then strip off all the leaves left on the plants and destroy them. Then we spray with a dormant oil preparation to keep down next year's diseases and pests." She and Jon attend meetings and conventions on their new passion whenever they can, and their interest in roses goes beyond the antiques. She strays from that criteria when something beautiful catches her eye. A few modern roses have sneaked into the mix, including the 1945 'Peace'. "I'm nothing like some of those antique collectors," Spieler says. "I'm not a purist; I want them all."

126

THE COLLECTOR'S GARDEN

ABOVE LEFT: *Portals give a glimpse of the walled garden as visitors walk to the front door. A bench by the house settles beneath an arbor covered with the climbing rose, 'Mermaid',* ABOVE RIGHT, *and creamy-pearl 'Mme. Alfred Carrière'.* OPPOSITE: *A close-up of this exquisite rose exhibits the sumptuous elegance of the old-fashioned varieties.*

Perhaps there should be a sign outside of Paul Keisling's Massachusetts garden: "Warning: Experienced gardener under controlled conditions. Do not attempt this at home!"

Responsible garden writers are reluctant to ever talk about hardy terrestrial orchids except when cautioning about their endangered status and suggesting that no one should buy them unless the species desired is among the more propagatable ones, from a source such as a botanical garden or wildflower society. They are nearly impossible to transplant because, among other reasons, of a symbiotic mycorrhizal relationship—they must grow with a specific fungus in the soil.

Keisling, an amateur gardener, grows these plants, defying convention, and grows them well. The clumps of allegedly impossible-to-grow orchids are lush with foliage and resplendent with blooms in mid-spring. He can because his research, along with the application of observations by other experts, including Dr. Frederick Case (pages 67–69), Dr. Richard Lighty of Mount Cuba Center, and Bill Brumback of the New England Wildflower Society, has led him to provide ideal conditions for his charges. Keisling knows that the trick is in replicating virtual duplicates of the plant's original homesites.

A case in point could be *Cypripedium guttatum* var. *yatabeanum* from the Aleutian Islands, where it

It would be simple enough to warn gardeners not to grow any of the threatened plants shown on these pages. But conservationists like Paul Keisling are dedicated to finding ways to cultivate and propagate them out of their habitats and thereby save them if their homes are developed. OPPOSITE: Cypripedium macranthum *var.* hotei-artsumorianum. ABOVE LEFT: C. calceolus *var.* pubescens. *Sometimes spectacular jewels such as C. calceolus are protected in humble cages of expedient design,* ABOVE RIGHT.

grows in cool loam and full sun. In a warm soil microorganisms would thrive that could kill it. Keisling prepared a soil mix of gravel and clay with little organic matter to feed soil bacteria. He planted the orchids among large rocks to keep their roots cool and under a canopy of deciduous trees. To compensate for the nearly sterile soil, he feeds with a diluted orchid fertilizer, and mulches with polyethylene.

For the plants that want a boggy environment, he makes his own. He scoops out the existing soil to a depth of about 18 inches, and as wide as needed for the desired planting. The hole is then lined with 6-millimeter polyethylene. Several holes are punched in the bottom to allow water to drain out slowly so that fertilizer salts don't build up in the boggy medium. He then fills the hole with a mixture of equal parts sand and sphagnum peat, which he thoroughly moistens.

To satisfy the orchids that want an alkaline environment, he mixes fine sand and good-quality garden loam, in equal amounts, and chunks of hardened horticultural lime to bring the pH up to about 8. The soil mix is mounded about a foot above the ground to keep the drainage good.

He has many *Cypripedium acaule,* the pink lady's-slipper orchid, that have been moved from around his property to the garden area. He claims that the success for them is not just the symbiotic fungal agent, but acidity, and places them in an area that gets natural runoff from granite rocks that helps to acidify the soil. "Acid is more important than water for these plants," he says, and after so much success with such difficult and misunderstood dependents, he should know.

By studying their habitats, Keisling has discovered the light, soil, moisture, and acidity requirements of his many hardy terrestrial orchids, believing that the only obstacle to their wider popularity is the development of mass-propagation methods. Cypripedium japonicum *var.* Formosanum, ABOVE, *likes a boggy location.* OPPOSITE: *The amazing lime-green flowers of* C. henryi.

Marionette' was the first daylily I ever planted," says Sydney Eddison about a 1950 egg-yolk-yellow flower with a handsome dark-red eye. "I didn't dare buy the most expensive, up-to-date hybrids then. But even the moderately priced cultivars thrilled me. I used to go mad every spring when the half-price sales were advertised." Today, Eddison's Connecticut garden is dominated by a long perennial border filled with carefully selected and beautifully grown blossoming plants. You would never imagine that among these sparkling colors are nearly 200 cultivars of *Hemerocallis* (daylily), the genus that has enchanted her for more than thirty years.

Eddison is very keen on the daylily's history, having fallen in love with what she considers "American plants." Of course, daylilies originated in Asia and were grown in Europe, but they blossomed here, horticulturally speaking. A lot of the credit goes to the father of daylily breeders, Dr. A. B. Stout, who during his years at the New York Botanical Garden made some fifty thousand crosses.

"America has the best climate for them," says Eddison, who wrote *A Passion for Daylilies,* about professional and amateur hybridizers. "They can tolerate cold and, even better, heat." Some of the foremost breeders live near Chicago, for example, where winter-to-summer temperature spans 130 degrees F.

Sydney Eddison has such a passion for her specialty, daylilies, that she wrote a book about them, but she does not believe these collectibles must be isolated from other plants. She grows more than 150 kinds in a long perennial border at her Connecticut home, ABOVE. OPPOSITE, CLOCKWISE FROM TOP LEFT *(all flowers pictured are in scale to one another):* 'Yesterday Memories'; 'Pearl Lewis'; 'Little Vine Spider'; 'Little Grapette'; 'Siloam Button Box'; 'Hot Embers'.

Unlike many of the 6,000 members of the American Hemerocallis Society, Eddison uses daylilies as garden plants—something collectors forget once the bug to possess every new cultivar bites. A familiar one in old-fashioned gardens such as Eddison's is 'Hyperion', a fragrant pale-yellow flower introduced by Franklin B. Mead of Fort Wayne, Indiana, in 1925. There are two large clumps in her border.

Eddison's passion has had several chapters. By the 1970s, she had *discovered* the tetraploids. Breeders found that by exposing seeds to a chemical derived from an autumn crocus (*Colchicum autumnale*), they could produce plants with thick *scapes* (flower stalks) and many more fleshy flowers. At first they became the fad, but now the trend is moving away from the pumped-up plants. Eddison hides their foliage behind other plants to get the benefit of the megaflowers without the hefty foliage.

In the 1980s, she started to lust after the miniatures. Today, she seems to love the old and the new equally, and is as pleased with the flat-faced, ruffle-edged, spider-petaled, or perfect pink newcomers as she is with the heirlooms. "Some still have their original labels," she says about certain old plants in her collection. "Others I know by heart, and quite a few remain beloved but anonymous."

At 6:00 P.M. on a summer's eve she begins a practice that might drive some mad, but is to her an act of devotion—blossom breaking, or deadheading. Instead of dealing with the mushy flowers in the morning of the next day, she snaps them off and carries them to what must be the most colorful compost heap in the area. How long does it take Eddison to break blossoms each evening? "One and half hours; but I love it. It's my time of day to really examine the plants and the garden. My moment for Zen meditation." She wouldn't have it any other way.

ABOVE LEFT: *The backyard garden can be reached by stone steps around the side of the house. There, a daylily is used as a landscape specimen with honeysuckle vine,* Lonicera × heckrottii. ABOVE RIGHT: *Behind the perennial border is a shaded collection of hostas, a plant that many* Hemerocallis *fanciers also acquire.* OPPOSITE, CLOCKWISE FROM TOP LEFT *(flowers in scale):* 'Shining Plumage'; 'Joan Senior'; 'Sweet Harmony'; unknown Munson cultivar; 'Corky'; 'Malaysia Monarch'.

Rick Darke, Curator of Plants at Longwood Gardens in Pennsylvania, is well aware that his specialty, ornamental grasses, has a potential to escape the garden and colonize open spaces. He is a conservationist dedicated to the preservation of native species and habitats. "I'm often asked to consult on design jobs," he says, "and sometimes I have to tell people that what they intend to plant might be beautiful, but if they grow it next to a field or meadow, it will take over."

In the landscape Darke shares with horticulturist Melinda Zoehrer, he has removed many of the most aggressive self-sowers. He advises gardeners not to plant certain ones and has systematically investigated the grass family to discover sterile varieties and natives to take the place of some of the more popular offenders. For example, he suggests growing the sterile hybrid *Calamagrostis acutiflora* 'Karl Foerster', feather-reed grass, a widely available, easy plant that has erect cream-colored seedheads persisting into early winter. The upright flowers begin to appear in late spring and start out feathery purple and eventually become about 30 inches tall. They move constantly in the wind and arch in rain, but always return to their vertical stance.

Darke has also never seen *Miscanthus sinensis* 'Purpurescens' produce viable seed that could spread. It is an early bloomer that also has the best red-orange fall color of any of the *Miscanthus,* but only grows to about 5 feet tall. For people who want something even taller, he recommends a native, such as

137

Rick Darke designed his garden to take advantage of light—especially the long, low rays of autumn, when the garden peaks with interest from river birch (Betula nigra *'Heritage'*) *with curling bark,* ABOVE LEFT, *and grasses, Darke's passion, such as* Calamagrostis acutiflora *'Karl Foerster',* ABOVE RIGHT, *and* Miscanthus sinensis *'Purpurescens',* OPPOSITE, *two grasses that do not self-sow.*

Panicum virgatum (switch grass or panic grass), which is found in nearly all states east of Nevada. The selection *P. virgatum* 'Cloud Nine' grows 6 feet or more. The cultivar *P. virgatum* 'Heavy Metal' is becoming very popular for its steely-blue foliage.

Andropogon gerardii (big bluestem) is also quite tall—up to 6 feet, quite blue, as is its close relative *Schizachyrium scoparium* (little bluestem), which grows through much of the central and eastern United States. *Sorghastrum nutans* (Indiangrass) has blue foliage, too, and rust-and-gold tassel flowers. It is native from Arizona eastward. *Muhlenbergia rigens* (deer grass) is an excellent western native. Its flowers remain ornamental right through to spring. *M. lindheimeri* (big muhly) shows even greater potential as an ornamental for southern and western states. As with most of the grasses, the season of interest reaches its height in the autumn when Darke's garden peaks.

The tawny dried grass glistens in the sun, a fact Darke knows well. This is one of the few gardens whose principle design was light. He actually plants for effects of light through the seasons and hours of the day. "I know we'll be walking from the driveway to the house after work, so I planted grasses and trees with peeling bark to be backlighted by the afternoon sun," he says.

Native woody plants for this season are also an interest of Darke's. "I love *Fothergilla major* and *F. gardenii* with leaves in all different colors at once," he says. *Hydrangea quercifolia* (oakleaf hydrangea) has dried flowers that last through the winter. Native azaleas are among the fall-interest woody plants he collects along with several species of *Halesia* (silver bell), which have attractive dangling seedpods.

Among his jobs as a curator at Longwood is to evaluate many of the plants that pass through. He is always inquisitive, always looking for the best in any new plant. But unlike some of the grass lovers, he keeps an open mind and has a keen understanding of the tenuous place of grass in ornamental horticulture and the delicate balance of nature.

Autumn color comes from the red and burgundy foliage of oakleaf hydrangea (Hydrangea quercifolia) *and the puffy seedheads of* Aster divaricatus, ABOVE. OPPOSITE: Lindera angustifolia *holds its cinnamon-colored leaves through winter.*

Creeks still run through Walnut Creek, California, but the trees have all but disappeared from a place named for the groves since supplanted by suburban sprawl. Only Ruth Bancroft's property remains from a huge plantation developed over a century ago by her late husband's grandfather. When the last of four acres of the declining trees were taken down in 1971, Bancroft's husband had an unusual idea: that she bring some of the special plants she had nurtured over the years in a series of greenhouses, lathe houses, and cold frames out into the open, and make a garden of them.

There had always been traditional gardens around the Bancroft house—a lawn, rose garden, and perennial border—but the new place was to be different. It was to be a collector's garden, and with Lester Hawkins (cofounder of Western Hills, pages 91–95), she developed a design.

The distinct theme to Bancroft's famous garden, whose subtext is precision and passion, is *xerophytes*—plants of dryland habitats. She collects cacti and succulents from the world's deserts and grows them to perfection in a loamy topsoil that has a lot of sand and humus worked in—they require exacting culture. More than a place to nurture plants, this was to be a designed garden, first and foremost. On a four-acre site, it isn't easy to create intimacy. These sculptural specimens are best seen

Ruth Bancroft's garden is remarkable not only for the sheer numbers of succulents, but for the design—a series of islands, ABOVE, *that visitors eagerly explore to find what lies around the next corner. This is a morphology collection of plants that store moisture in their fleshy tissues, such as* Agave stricta, OPPOSITE. FOLLOWING PAGES: *Blue* Agave franzosinii.

close up—their spiky forms, back-lit spines, or blue foliage have to be visually felt to be experienced.

The clever construction of the beds created a series of islands of trees, shrubs, cacti, and succulents. A friend, the collector of South African bulbs, Stan Farwig, describes a visit to this place as a voyage—an oxymoronic metaphor for a garden whose only apparent water lies in a man-made oasis. But here visitors sail smoothly along the paths, around the edges of the planted beds, and slowly, bit by bit, the next island is revealed. In this way, every inch can be savored before the whole is seen.

If this design, which shows off plants as well as any museum displays its artworks, seems a bit of a contrivance, then consider the exacting process necessary to keep these precious individuals alive. Walnut Creek, about 25 miles east of San Francisco, is not a desert. The summer weather is fine for the succulents, but the winter is not. It rains and can get too cold.

The solution is coldframes, about three hundred of them made of wood and polyethylene, ranging from 1 single cubic foot to 20. The frames are set out in October and remain in place until April. "It takes about three weeks to place them all around the garden," says Bancroft.

Every quarter-century has its killer freeze, when gardens that push the coastal California climate often have to start from scratch, and one occurred here not too long ago. "We lost hundreds of plants," admits Bancroft, though her collection of one thousand bearded iris varieties, planted as a river of

All of the structures in the Bancroft garden, trellises, frames for winter covering, and the like, are painted her signature verdigris. The large lathe house was designed like a Victorian Palm House with wings. The center of the building serves as the main entrance to the garden. In the foreground is a bed of blue-green Aloe striata *with hot red-orange flowers.*

The range and scope of the forms of plants and their flowers in the Bancroft garden seem limitless. Many beg to be stroked and petted, but there's the rub—needles and spines are the price of beauty and protection for the botanical charges here. CLOCKWISE FROM TOP LEFT: Agave americana *'Variegata';* Cleistocactus hylacanthus; Eriogonum umbellatum *var.* poly-anthum; *the giant bromeliad,* Puya chilensis; Senecio mandraliscae; Drosanthemum speciosum; Opun-tia *spp. in front of* Yucca aloifolia *'Marginata'; the white flowers of* Trichocereus schickendantzii.

color, flourished. The succulent garden made a remarkable comeback, and after renovation, has never looked better. The structures—including the elaborate entrance to the garden, a lathe house fashioned like one of the great palm-house conservatories of the Victorian era—and even utilitarian features have been reconditioned and freshly painted the color of the garden-architecture's leitmotif: verdigris.

The uniqueness of this collection, its remarkable presentation, and sheer beauty led to a great honor. In 1989, Frank Cabot, one of America's premier plant collectors and gardeners, founded an organization dedicated to the preservation of American gardens. *The Garden Conservancy*, as it is called, chose Ruth Bancroft's garden as the first to be taken under its wing.

Views around the garden. OPPOSITE, CLOCKWISE FROM TOP LEFT: *The oasis pool at the center of the garden edged with* Echeverias *and featuring yellow flag* (Iris pseudacorus); *golden barrel cactus* (Echinocactus grusonii); *a view of the garden maker's house; an ancient* Agave *flops like a giant squid taking a siesta.* ABOVE, CLOCKWISE FROM TOP LEFT: Opuntia spp; *a collection of cacti and succulents exhibiting their varied colors and textures; the exquisite cactus flowers of* Trichocereus schickendantzii; *flowering* Crassula anomala *with* Sedum cauticola.

B y now, the story of Jim Cross's leap into the wholesale nursery business is well known. While still a successful Wall Street executive in the 1960s, he began to grow plants on the North Fork of Long Island, New York; then, around 1970, he abandoned New York City to make his avocation a full-time job. Today, Environmentals is one of the best-known suppliers of dwarf woody plants, and Jim Cross has become an inspiration to many in the field.

About ten years after Cross left the city, a feisty New Yorker who was in the indoor plant trade happened by. She owned a business giving plant parties: selling decorative interior landscape plants in people's homes. Conni Rosiello came to Environmentals to shop, stayed to work, and ended up marrying the boss. Today, her design business, independent of the nursery, is thriving.

The Crosses are marvelously complementary—he, the coolheaded, contemplative plantsman; she, the animated, opinionated artist. Together, they have had more of an effect on promoting environmentally sensitive ornamental horticulture in their area than anybody. They always have a crusade: water conservation, responsible resource management, and the quest to get new plants into the market.

"Americans are looking for different plants," says Jim. "It's natural that they'll want interesting ones, and necessary that these be more compact for lower maintenance and to save space." This is one reason why there are *Daphne* species at garden centers today. Jim Cross has nearly single-handedly taken some of these former rock-garden curiosities—recognizing them as useful garden plants—and propagated them for the general garden enthusiast. One example is *Daphne* × *burkwoodii* 'Carol Mackie'; dis-

OPPOSITE: *A rustic gazebo overlooks three pools in a new garden that features a black urn and frothy chartreuse* Alchemilla mollis *flowers.* ABOVE LEFT: Hydrangea paniculata *'Tardiva' is a low-growing cultivar with dense floral panicles that also bloom earlier than the more common H. p. 'Grandiflora', or PeeGee hydrangea.* ABOVE RIGHT: *The path in front of the house leads to a garden pot nestled among shaded hostas and ferns beneath a cut-leaf Japanese maple.*

covered in its namesake's New Jersey garden, it is a semievergreen variegated gray-green and cream-leafed spring blooming shrub that grows to 4 feet tall. It has pink buds that open to fragrant stars. A newer one, something to look for in the future, is *Daphne caucasica.* This easy shrub is actually everblooming—presenting fragrant flowers in every month of the growing season: spring through fall.

For decades, Cross has collected dwarf evergreens, and now many of these specimens make an impressive sight to see—especially outside of a botanical garden. There are mature 10-foot *Chamaecyparis pisisera* cultivars with weeping branches, wide-spreading colorful mounds of *Juniperus horizontalis* cultivars, tall silvery *Picea abies,* and massive mats of *Pinus strobus* 'Prostrata', barely 12 inches tall.

The gardens that the Crosses have made at their homesite just behind the nursery are pure American. They are very much a reflection of their owners—perhaps mostly of Conni, but Jim advises about which plants to be used, sometimes vetoing a choice, more often making a suggestion.

Conni Cross is well known for color combinations with annuals and perennials mixed with flowering shrubs, evergreens, and even houseplants. Much of her work has a diminutive quality, almost a whimsy, but she is also quite astute. A heather and heath garden planted in a mound of pure sand and a nearly xerophytic lawn rooted in soil to which tons of organic matter were added are just a couple of her inspired concoctions.

One of the most beautiful areas of their property is the swimming-pool garden, surrounded by more exquisite, unusual evergreens—many introduced because Jim Cross recognized their potential and propagated them to offer through Environmental's extensive catalog. Looking at the exhaustive listing, someone once asked him what his favorite plants were. "The last six I saw," he answered.

ABOVE: *The pool has a naturalistic design and is surrounded by rocks and stone paving to blend into its setting. These gardens are for people and must function as outdoor living spaces as well as displays of herbaceous perennials and rare conifer collections.*

CLOCKWISE FROM TOP LEFT: *A trip through the Cross property begins with the first garden to bloom—the alpine collection next to the bedroom window starts in the winter; the view from this garden looking in the opposite direction toward the mounded heathers and heaths at the other end of the house; members of the woody plant collection including a golden Juniperus chinensis 'Old Gold'; the lawn in front of the playhouse where violas are allowed to bloom in the grass; the variegated dwarf conifer Tsuga canadensis 'Albospica' next to a birdhouse; one of the three garden pools with Hosta 'Gold Standard' and, blooming, H. 'Blue Cadet'; the rustic gazebo; the path to the nursery is lined with woody and herbaceous plants including lilies.*

Jim Waddick's garden and the space behind the home of his partner, Jim Murrain, next door, have some of the most spectacular plants seen anywhere. The "Jims'" collections, all in about 2,500 square feet, include very strange-looking plants, along with fascinating versions of familiar plants. The focus is on foliage permutations, with an eye to newly discovered plants, *Iris* species, and variegated anything. "We're both fond of weeds and variegated plants," says Waddick, "and the variegated weeds are the best."

This unconventional garden concentrates on discovery, acquisition, experimentation, cultivation, observation, distribution, and then—maybe—design. It is a collection in the truest sense of the word, and because of the possibility of a hasty relocation, much of what is there has "gone to pot and into pots," as Waddick puts it.

Even under such space constraint, the searching continues. "We wander up and down rows of nurseries looking for something odd, especially variegated," says Murrain, "even if it's a variegated marigold among ten thousand seedlings." Sometimes the searches take Waddick farther afield. "Around six years ago, I became interested in *Iris,*" he says, "especially beardless species. Several friends were sitting around the dining table, and we were saying it must be really easy to get someone who knows about iris to hop on a plane and collect species now that China has opened up. Talk about naive. That person turned out to be me!"

Through an arduous trip that did not involve the better accommodations or government-guided tours, Waddick managed to bring out more Chinese-species *Iris* than had ever been seen in the West. He's been back—most recently to collect a magnolia. "When they told me there was a 40-foot-tall *Magnolia* species in China that had never been introduced, I couldn't believe it, but it's true," he says. "And there's a hellebore that we've been watching to collect seed at just the right moment. *Helleborus*

153

Jim Waddick is so fascinated with color in leaves that he will collect just about any plant that exhibits some variation in its foliage. Satisfying his obsession can sometimes mean paying for the privilege, but fortunately the expensive Canna 'Durban', OPPOSITE, *was a gift.* ABOVE, LEFT TO RIGHT: Oenanthe javanica *'Flamingo';* Iris pallida *'Aurea Variegata';* Tovara virginiana *'Variegata'.*

thibetanus seeds are viable for such a short time. A colleague there has been standing by to collect the seeds and send them to be germinated during the small window of opportunity."

From China, he has also brought a *Saxifraga stolonifera* (strawberry begonia) form that is bigger, more vigorous, and hardier than the one grown in European and North American gardens. He has helped to collect some new species of the genus *Lycoris* (naked-ladies). Growers are now experimenting with these, and soon the new ones will be offered from places like the Daffodil Mart, Plant Delights, and even the mainstream mail-order nursery White Flower Farm.

Another plant group that Waddick favors shows commercial promise—the bowl lotus, so called because they are tiny in comparison to normal *Nelumbo* species and cultivated in bowls in the Orient. They could be grown in a small water garden, on a deck, or balcony.

The astonishing collection includes a grasslike *Carex siderosticha* 'Variegata', a variegated *Datura* the two men found in a field and have been propagating, and a variegated *Helleborus orientalis*. *Kerria japonica* 'Kin-Kan' has white and green stems—wonderful for winter interest. The leaves are solid green, but the canes are striped. There is a variegated ginkgo tree along with other unusual woody plants, including a variegated rose of Sharon and a lilac rescued by a woman who worked for a local breeder.

One of my favorites is a magnificent variegated *Viburnum lantana*. It has felted leaves spattered with yellow that age to white, but new growth is always coming, and always shows yellow. Waddick has offered it to wholesale nurseries to propagate, but no one seems interested—astonishing, since this handsome specimen easily tolerates Kansas City's continental climate that often gets to 100-plus degrees F in the summer, and reliably hits −10 in the winter—sometimes −20.

Is there any variegated plant Waddick doesn't like? "Yes," he says, "*Petasites japonica* 'Variegata' (butterbur)." But, of course, he grows that, too. He even has a delicate rose, its leaves terrifically spattered with white. "It's often sold as 'Wichuraiana', but don't be fooled," he says. It's that nasty *Rosa multiflora*, a tough environmental menace in many regions. But fortunately, this one is a wimp in Kansas City. "It barely makes it through the winter," says Murrain. "We cut it back and hope for the best, and usually get a plant to grow up the fence a bit." It's just another favorite weed.

Variegation, once a laughing matter among gardeners, is now an obsession for many collectors who are excited because these plants are just beginning to be offered. Waddick helped found ABG—Anything But Green—inspired by plants such as, ABOVE, LEFT TO RIGHT: Viburnum lantana *'Variegata';* Arum italicum *'Pictum'; and a variegated* Asarum canadensis, *which owes its transient beauty to a virus.*

CLOCKWISE FROM TOP LEFT:
Polygonum cuspidatum *Variegatum*;
Rubus fruticosa *Albovariegata*; Viola
sororia *Albovariegata*; Pleioblastus
viridistriatus; Duchesnea indica
Variegata; *a form of* Helleborus viridis;
Carex elata *Aurea* (*Bowles' golden sedge*);
Aralia elata *Aurea Variegata*; *a* Saxifraga
stolonifera *found by Waddick in China*;
Rosa wichuraiana *Variegata*. ABOVE:
Asarum inflatum.

Mountainous areas high above the timberline have always had a certain attraction for Lee Raden, but replicating an alpine landscape for a garden near Philadelphia was a daunting prospect. Soil, rock, and drainage conditions can be approximated, but the summers in eastern Pennsylvania are hot and humid—deadly to alpine plants. Still, Raden perseveres, fooling his beloved phloxes and hawkweeds into growing pretty much as they do in nature. His virtual-reality replicas of alpine meadows are the crowning achievement.

An expert rock gardener and rare-plant enthusiast, Raden has exhibited in the Philadelphia Flower Show for thirty years—forcing plants into bloom for display in March. In the greenhouse behind his home, many unusual rock and woodland plants wait for their debut in the show or the garden. Despite the challenges of his collection—ice storms, power failures, and the humidity outdoors that seems to melt his favorite specimens—he remains one of the most enthusiastic gardeners I have ever met.

"I owe it all to two women," says Raden. He and his wife received a wedding gift certificate for the nearby nursery of *Primula* and *Viola* expert Doretta Klaber, from a family friend, Elizabeth Nimmo. "Doretta's woods were filled with primroses. Oh, it was a sight." Klaber convinced him to start a Delaware Valley Chapter of the North American Rock Garden Society (for which he served as president). That was thirty years ago, and it is still one of the most active chapters in the organization. "When I began, I didn't know a tree from a blade of grass. Klaber and Nimmo were my mentors."

157

Most of Lee Raden's property is woodland, but the front of his house is a collector's garden inspired by a habitat—alpine meadows—only here at sea level in Pennsylvania. Phlox and conifers flourish on the "hills," OPPOSITE. *He has also made gravel scree,* ABOVE.

His first garden concentrated on a collection of conifers, and he still has many choice, rare specimens, such as *Juniperus rigida, J. conferta, J. wiltonii,* and a *Pinus parviflora* 'Bergmanii' that might be the oldest specimen alive. He will never part with it, and it probably could not survive transplantation, but his friend, Julia Morris, the horticulturist at Blithewold Arboretum in Bristol, Rhode Island, has a standing offer. "If she sells it for over $100,000, she gets 25 percent." This is barely a joke. In 1976, Raden traded 300 of his shrubs for the 2½ acres where he built this house and garden.

Raden knew he had a special affinity for the windswept mountain meadows, and he purposefully set out to make them on machine-built hummocks in his front yard. They are made of a blend of topsoil, stream sand, and tons of pebbles and rocks. He did not mix the medium too well, but that makes for varying conditions—not unlike the true rocky alpine soil. Plants grow taller in the richer areas and more dwarf in the leaner sections, which includes native columbines, *Aquilegia canadensis,* ranging in height from about 6 to 24 inches.

For several weeks in midspring, the garden is an undulating canvas of white, apple-blossom pink, cerise, and lavender—the peak of his collection of ground-hugging phlox. Raden started primarily with three phloxes—*Phlox procumbens, P. subulata* and *P. bifida*—and they have crossed. Plants are everywhere, even in the gravel edges at the base of the hummocks, which are like a natural *scree* (the stony debris at the base of a mountain), a perfect seedbed for alpines. In one area *Hieracium waldsteinii,* "a marvelous hawkweed," is just coming up. "Just like in the paths through the mountains, plants are growing in the gravel," he says, his ideal realized.

The paths are essential for Raden's sense of achievement. "It's a walking garden, you can go anywhere," he says. "It really takes you away. Every day is so exciting—all of a sudden, something pops open and floods the air with overpowering perfume. I fantasize. I close my eyes and I'm somewhere else, I don't know exactly where, but I feel I've been there before."

OPPOSITE: *The phlox have interbred to create myriad colors in tidy mats in the scree.* ABOVE LEFT: *A striped* Phlox subulata *'Tamanongalei' from Woodbank Nursery in Tasmania. Native red* Aquilegia canadensis *self-sows throughout,* ABOVE RIGHT.

Plain, unadulterated plant greed led me to rock gardening," says Gwen Kelaidis of Denver, Colorado. "New beds, new plants arriving in cardboard boxes, hundreds of new plants germinating in tray after tray. It was thrilling, it was glorious, it was heaven!"

Though today she is a preeminent collector of alpines, she came to gardening through the vegetable patch, as many gardeners do, then on to colorful flowering annuals. Next it was perennials. She pored over the works of Gertrude Jekyll and made plans for sweeps of color. But the desire to grow more plants than would fit into plantings based on masses of flowers all-of-a-kind ruled out the traditional border.

For fifteen years, Gwen Kelaidis searched for a justification for her collector's appetite. Science provided some rationalizations. She figured that plants in nature grow according to their destinies. Plants that colonize space have a *uniform* distribution. Ones that flow in sweeps are said to have *aggregate* arrangement. Plants that have no apparent pattern are *random*. Vegetable gardening favors a uniform plan. Perennial borders owe much to aggregate characteristics. But rock gardening, and Gwen Kelaidis's style, is random like the tundra—many different plants growing in a somewhat spare, albeit promiscuous, jumble. Still, she searched for an *artistic* metaphor to describe her garden.

"Garden design has never been my strong point," she wrote in a recent issue of the *North American Rock Garden Society Bulletin,* which she edits. "I am a doer sort of person. I can sow seed, transplant, dig, mix soil, move rocks, shovel manure, gravel or sand, and plant plants—but design has always given me pause." She suddenly realized that her creations were like Persian carpets with similar colors and arrangements as the rugs. There are limited tones in the carpets in related families—shades of wine and brown or tan and cream—much like the foliage and flowers of the tiny plants she grows. Kelaidis

OPPOSITE: *Gwen and Panayoti Kelaidis's suburban Denver backyard is filled with berms, or hummocks. By turning the ground on end, Gwen has enormously increased the planting area. Not only do the hummocks have four sunlight exposures, they also are dry at the top and moist at the bottom to afford specific conditions for literally thousands of alpines such as* Saxifraga paniculata, ABOVE LEFT, *and* Onosma alboroseum, ABOVE RIGHT.

collects alpines, specifically plants of the Rocky Mountain steppes and the steppes of Eurasia, which inspired the carpet makers as well. "The background colors of the carpets are not unlike the grasses of the central Asian meadows, or the mineral soils of the steppes, or my gravel mulch," she points out.

Her backyard is populated by berms, or hummocks, piles of amalgam, upon which her tiny rock plants reside. Because she views these plantings more or less straight on, she knew that she wasn't making impressionistic plantings in three dimensions, as do perennial-border makers, but flat tapestries.

The berms serve many purposes. For one thing, they make a whole lot of gardening space in a backyard of just over 1,000 square feet. By building berms, she made a garden that, flattened out, would be huge, but grows up instead of out, with plants hugging the sides of undulating, amorphous pyramids. The berms also add a north, south, east, and west exposure to every planting and create diverse moisture conditions. "It's like a sponge saturated with water. When you set the sponge on end, the top becomes rather dry, and the bottom becomes wet. The berms have this aspect, too, so I can grow plants that want more moisture at the bottom and less at the top."

The front and backyard gardens feature thousands of plants. The xeric front favors sunproof colors of orange and red and has become known in the area as an example of a planting that requires no extra water to survive. Both front and back gardens feature one genus for which Kelaidis and her husband, Panayoti (page 9), are well known—*Eriogonum*—the wild buckwheats, a group of plants that have barely been examined and are rarely grown, something the Kelaidises are going to change.

The genus *Eriogonum* has nearly 250 species, mostly found in the Western states. They are low-growing tufts with flowers above the silver-gray foliage. As the flowers age, the coloration changes, showing subtle yellow, gradations of brilliant orange to red and rust—like a Persian carpet whose colors grow richer with age.

The Kelaidises are devoted to alpine plants from the Rocky Mountains. They are also passionate about a genus they believe will become a popular garden plant: Erigonum. *Many species grow in the front yard,* OPPOSITE. *Called wild buckwheats, they are generally low mats with elevated floral umbels that often start out one color and change hue and shade.* ABOVE: Eriogonum umbellatum *'Altura Red',* LEFT, *and two color forms of* Eriogonum caespitosum, RIGHT.

here's something about woodland gardening I simply adore," says Judy Glattstein, a well-known teacher of horticulture and a garden-book author. "But then, there's nothing like the prairie; and Japanese gardens are incredible; and . . ."

It is not just one aspect of horticulture that Glattstein loves, but all gardens and plants. When she first saw her Connecticut home in 1976, it was not the house that attracted her, but the trees behind it—a wonderful wooded hollow with the kind of soil that only time and fortune can make. It is an incredible humus-rich amalgam of years of fallen oak leaves, with excellent drainage—the dream situation for anyone who wants to collect shade-loving wildflowers from the world's temperate regions.

This is not a designed garden, but more of a stage set for experimentation, where the colorplay lasts from February to November. Glattstein seems to learn from nature's accidents as much as from what her will imposes. "I'm fascinated to see what plants do rather than what you've intended," she says.

Her primary directive is to site a plant perfectly in terms of its cultural needs, but when a *Phlox divaricata* (wild sweet William) winds its way around an *Athyrium japonicum* 'Pictum' (Japanese painted fern) and the colors seem perfect together—so be it. There are seedling *Helleborus* species with *Pulmonaria* species (lungworts), *Trillium erectum* 'Album' with *Brunnera macrophylla* (Siberian bugloss), *Lunaria annua*

165

Judy Glattstein loves all gardens but is most partial to the woodland habitat. She collects plants that like these conditions. In spring, one area is brilliant with chartreuse from the new growth of ferns and hostas, and Hakonechloa macra *'Aureola',* OPPOSITE. ABOVE: Helleborus orientalis *and* Pulmonaria rubra *flowers,* LEFT; Dicentra *'Purity' and* Trillium cuneatum, RIGHT.

(moneyplant) and *Narcissus poeticus* 'Actaea' (poet's narcissus). *Pachysandra procumbens* (Allegheny spurge), *Podophyllum peltatum* (May apple), *Matteuccia pennsylvanica* (ostrich fern), and *Epimedium* subspecies (bishop's-hat) weave together with *Hosta* 'Krossa Regal', which echoes the vase form of the ostrich fern a few paces away. Rare, single-flowered *Paeonia japonica* teams with *Hosta* 'Ginkgo Craig', *Rodgersia* species, *Myrrhis odorata,* and a self-sown *Euonymus.*

Just imagine a bed of Japanese painted fern instead of impatiens, none of which are found in this shaded garden. Instead, there are *Trillium grandiflorum, T. cuneatum, T. erectum, T. erectum* 'Album', *T. sessile, T. luteum,* and *Arisaema thunbergii* 'Urashima', *A. ringens, A. candidissima,* and several versions of our native *A. triphyllum* (Jack-in-the pulpit). Some taxonomists do not believe that there are different varieties, but Glattstein does. She shows the distinctions between ones such as *A. triphyllum* 'Sterwardsonii' with clearly raised pale ridges and *A. t.* 'Zebrinum', with white stripes on the dark purple spathe.

Another theme is to pair native species and their European and Asian counterparts, such as *Jeffersonia diphylla* from North America and *J. dubia* from Asia; the worldly North American and Asian *Arisaema; Astilbe biternata,* our native, and other *Astilbe* species; and even *Pachysandra procumbens* (Allegheny spurge) with the familiar *P. terminalis* (Japanese spurge).

In 1994, Glattstein learned her husband, Paul, was being relocated. She worried no home buyer would find her garden as interesting as she did; most likely, she speculated, they will replace her plantings with a swimming pool. "These are living creatures that I have nurtured for a long time and to find out they end up at the bottom of a swimming pool is a terrible thing." In defense of her progeny, she packed up as many as possible, hoping the next place would be as kind to them as this one.

Amazing plants grow in this woodland habitat garden, including some of the most sought-after and rare woodlanders such as Lilium tsingtauense, ABOVE LEFT, *and lilac-colored* Glaucidium palmatum, OPPOSITE. *Most* Glaucidium *come from society seed exchanges, but* Galanthus nivalis, ABOVE RIGHT, *from the genus for which Glattstein is best known, is widely available.*

Lauren Springer collects tough plants—not ones that are hard to culti-
vate, but ones that can take a licking and keep on growing. She wanted a dense, cottage-style garden
filled with the intricate color plays that are her forte. But she quickly discovered that Colorado's harsh
climate dictates more about what can grow than do taste and talent. So the search began.

"I love this climate," says Springer of the mile-high plateau at the base of the Rockies. She moved
to this third of an acre in 1989, and set out to make a garden. "I came here and there was so little
information, no book had been written," she says, "so I killed a ton of plants. People are very conser-
vative here, as well. They tell you the climate is not conducive to gardening." Panayoti Kelaidis (page
9), the curator of the rock garden at the Denver Botanic Garden, told her otherwise. "This is a great
place to garden," he said. "All you do is add water, or take it away by increasing drainage. After all, this
soil is not so different from the short grass prairie and the corn belt."

Springer also met with a lot more resistance than just naysayers: heat in the summer and cold in the
winter. By mid-July she had seen her garden ripped to shreds by hailstorms. After a bout of self-pity,
she made two new compost piles out of the carnage. But she also discovered that the natives in her
garden and the ones from areas accustomed to hail had barely been scratched. So she embarked on a

Lauren Springer has proved that you can garden extremely well in Colorado. Her front yard, OPPOSITE, *is unconventional:
instead of a lawn, she has planted a remarkable perennial show featuring colorful vignettes such as this one with* Berberis thunbergii *'Atropurpurea Nana' (B. t. 'Crimson Pygmy') and* Iris pumila, ABOVE RIGHT. *Some areas are never watered—again
a test of the climate and the plants. The "Hell Strip" grows between the sidewalk and the curb,* ABOVE LEFT.

new direction: to find and grow more plants in tune with her site. "The key to finding the right plants lies in knowing their origins," she has written in her book *The Undaunted Gardener* (1994). Today, she collects weather-resistant plants—ones that will stand the extremes in temperature, freakish weather, and the clear sun of high altitudes. Some successes, both culturally and or naturally, have been *calcareous* (lime-loving) plants—alpines, succulents, and ones with silver foliage. But she does not grow simply what works; she also demands that her tough plants be beautiful.

In fact, gardeners in the plains of Colorado can grow more herbaceous plants than can their counterparts in the northeast. Springer has concentrated on several genera and families: *Penstemon* (the beard tongues), *Oenothera* (evening primroses), *Malvaceae* (members of the mallow family), and *Labiatae* (the mint family), and combined them with a host of others that show them off to an advantage.

Penstemon is probably her favorite, and it presents some of the most promising garden subjects. Like so many plants that go on to become international favorites, *Penstemon* is American. "There are about 250 species—all but one from the United States," says Springer. "Probably 100 have garden potential. I grow about 15 striking ones, and 15 marginally okay ones. I love *P. grandiflorus,* because it has eucalyptuslike leaves, and the mat-forming *P. teucrioides* with blue flowers. I also love them because I love plants that are busy—always visited by insects, hummingbirds, and bees. I like a lot of bugs."

Her garden is "plant driven, ultimately," based on what she calls "high-density gardening." Basically, she wanted to test out every idea and every plant she could. "We're a herbaceous mecca here," says Springer of the climate she has come to understand.

ABOVE: *Another view of the Hell Strip with the house beyond.* OPPOSITE, CLOCKWISE FROM TOP LEFT: *A view of the Irish Garden, inspired by the time Springer spent apprenticing in Ireland; facing away from the Irish Garden; pots of alpines by the front steps; bearded iris,* Allium, *and low evergreens are some of the plants used to make the lush creation in a climate known for its stark landscape.*

OPPOSITE: *Laura Fisher combines unconventional plants, including oversized prairie natives, around her pool. Arundo donax 'Variegata' shoots up through the planting.* FAR LEFT: *The green-and-white* Aralia elata *'Variegata'.* LEFT: *Frothy purple smoke bush (Cotinus coggygria 'Purpureus'), tall* Thalictrum rochebrunianum, *and purple cone flower* (Echinacea purpurea). ABOVE: Melianthus major.

Aesthetes

Most collectors define their collections by what they have, and search for what they don't have. One may need to complete a genus collection with a few more species; another seeks a never-before-grown alpine. There are others, however, who buy or grow plants just because they find them beautiful.

They are aesthetes, the last group presented, because these gardeners bring together the collectors' passion, perception, pride—and the plants. Art is the province of the aesthete collectors. Plants are their medium.

Aesthetes have a special way of seeing that leads them to feature some plants alone, as striking specimens, and combine others to create special effects in the garden. They take a mental magnifying glass to every plant. With heightened awareness, they examine all aspects, and discover the inner beauty that distinguishes each one as extraordinary. Aesthetes notice the serration of a *Melianthus major* leaf, and imagine ways to exploit the sawtooth shadows it casts on its neighbors. They do not view the tiny flowers of the *Codonopsis clematidea* as incidental. They take a moment to lift a flower and peer inside to see what Marcia Donahue (pages 203–207) calls "nature's stained-glass windows." When fragrance fills the air, they trace the sweet or pungent molecules to their origin. When they feel a leaf, touch becomes an exploration of its ridges and valleys, the leaf's fuzzy felt texture, or slickly polished surface. Artists want to preserve these memories, and one way to do that is to possess the plant that looks and feels and smells the way they remember.

Through the demands and crusades of the aesthetes, plants that might be overlooked frequently become fashionable. An example is the popular chocolate cosmos (*Cosmos atrosanguineus*), whose brown flowers actually smell like cocoa. *Astrantia* species have scaly petals that a decade ago would not have been considered showy enough to include in any garden, but now are sought-after because of their subtlety. *Dierama* has delicate dangling pink blossoms that line animated, fishing-pole-like wands. It is now coveted. *Euphorbia* varieties are being discovered by gardeners in North America. Most of these succulents are from the tropical drylands of the world, but hardy, shrubby and herbaceous ones are bursting onto the market. There is a resurgence of interest in *Clematis*. But now, it is not just the familiar ones with giant flowers that are sought, but ones with weird tiny, brown or green nodding bells that are as curious as they are beautiful. Some people even collect clematis for their exquisite seedheads.

With artists' eyes, aesthetes divine the various characteristics of a plant and make it useful in ways other than the obvious. A dense evergreen shrub might be pruned into a unique shape to fulfill their needs. A vine could be cajoled into arching this way or that. A fragrant flower could introduce a garden experience or alter it. A tree with smooth bark is placed where it can be stroked on the way to a secluded bench. Unusual plants make this more possible than run-of-the-mill selections, and make our creations more personal and original.

There is no such thing as an ugly garden—gardens, like babies, are all beautiful to their parents. I rarely see a garden that has nothing to offer—especially when the gardener's enthusiasm is evident; and aesthete collectors are the most enthusiastic gardeners of all. But, I'm afraid, collectors can be snobs and dismiss gardens for other reasons. Many aesthetes may be bored by modern constructions that are considered well designed by most people. For example, gardens that don't incorporate plants into their schemes, or ones that use plants to make carpets of color.

Traditional formal gardens may or may not delight the aesthetes. We appreciate beauty, no matter the style, if the design speaks to our heads and hearts. Many historical plantings have a sculptural quality, such as Villa Lante in Italy or Hestercombe in England. Despite their scale, gardens such as Vaux-le-Vicomte in France or Stourhead in England communicate a personal vision. We all respond to the originality that makes art what it is.

Edith Eddleman is known for two gardens, her own, ABOVE, *and the borders at North Carolina State University Arboretum,* OPPOSITE. *Tiny plants grow in hers, along with pieces of art, such as an enameled copper fish. The arboretum's borders use jumbo plants and the occasional whimsical objet d'art, such as the amethyst gazing globes among foamy* Eupatorium rugosum.

The same originality that makes a garden special is what separates the aesthete collectors from other designers who plant to fulfill an architectural dream, or are concerned with how a decorative garden can enhance a guest's visit. Aesthetes are more concerned with the esoteric individuals that populate the garden than its overall appearance. The aesthetes have no rules to break as long as their plants thrive. These are the most personal creations imaginable. Aesthetes set their own measures of success. Either you like it or you don't.

Glenn Withey and Charles Price are well-known garden designers in the Pacific Northwest. But they are driven more by plant collection and garden making than by a quest for fame or fortune. The new Bellevue Botanical Garden near Seattle, which includes an enormous perennial border, is a labor of love—completely planted and maintained by volunteers. Withey and Price search out unusual plants for flower and foliage color. The mammoth border straddles a hillside, but every square yard could be analyzed and interpreted as a garden in itself. Leaf textures; architectural stems; big and little flowers; purple, silver, and gold foliage; and, very often, yellow flowers are the leitmotifs in this astounding planting.

Near Great Barrington, Massachusetts, Robin Norris and Barbara Bockbrader made a humble cutting garden. Bockbrader collects unusual annuals that might have potential as cut flowers. It looks very much like a vegetable garden—with striped rows of color—and some of the specimens are edible, but they are not grown for food. The peculiar but vividly colorful variegated corn, flowering kale, and purple okra have all been assembled solely for their beauty. This garden, set out in an orderly fashion as most vegetable or cutting gardens are, has a museumlike quality. Carefully lining up plants and clearly and accurately labeling them are aspects of refined curatorial collecting. To the collector, and even the aesthete collector, rigid rows make this place no less fascinating. The plants star.

Aesthetes, Collection, and Design

Some professional garden makers and critics see collecting and design as mutually exclusive. Stephen Anderton, Horticultural Officer for English Heritage in the North Region of Great Britain, rails against the passion of collecting for collecting's sake. He sees the best plants as the tools for the job, and collectors as having made the tools more important than the product. He feels public gardens that advertise the number of taxa in their collections are missing an important

The borders at the new Bellevue Botanical Garden, ABOVE AND OPPOSITE, BELOW, *are ambitious—hundreds of feet long and more than 50 feet deep. Something like this might not be so unusual in England, but the palette, and the fact that much of the color comes from leaves, exhibits a decidedly American slant.*

aspect of botanical display—design. "A collection is like a book of wallpapers or swatches of fabric," he says. "It is a source to be consulted before creating something new, from which you can choose materials to serve your aesthetic purpose." Plants are "the finishing touches" to garden design. But he isn't communicating to us die-hard amassers of plants.

There seems to be a prejudice against plants among some landscape architects who use as little living material as possible, relying instead on immutable elements such as stone paving and concrete benches. The aesthetes may not put design first, but are nonetheless aware of art—something garden designers tend to subordinate when they build walls, place ubiquitous benches with views of nowhere, and install acres of no-maintenance "hard-scape." Of course, a collection would be nearly impossible to maintain if a client was not directly involved. Obviously, plants die, especially if there is no one to care for them. Concrete never dies.

Psychologically, this may have to do with control and the desire to make a lasting statement that will ensure the garden creator's immortality. Collectors may have more of a sense of the moment. One may not be able to get away for a week in the summer, but this chore is not a curse, it is devotion. And yet, many of us do have a desire to make long-lasting art, maybe even out of plants. Guy Sternberg of Petersburg, Illinois, collects oak trees (he has over a hundred species), and because these plants live at least a human's lifetime, one might imagine that he is sympathetic to the hardscapers since his creation will last for centuries. But unlike an installation of mortar and stone, his will take decades to be realized. The same is true of an aesthete who plants trees to make an allée, or vines to smother an arch with fragrant flowers.

Seeing Is Believing

Is a collection of plants like so many paintings in search of a museum? It is true that most aesthete collectors are more concerned with choosing the right frame and its contents than with traffic patterns and architectural perspective. But they are not examining pared-down design practiced by those who create usable spaces for all kinds of people. The collector's garden is generally made by and for one person, and is meant to be shared with others who know how to see each tree despite the forest—not only the paintings in the museum, but perhaps the brush strokes as well. They are concerned more about sheltering their wards than the appearance or structure of the setting.

Stephen Anderton might be surprised and delighted to find that design and collecting are not always incompatible. Many aesthetes attempt to combine these devotions. Collector Laura Fisher and designer Hitch Lyman avidly accumulate anything they can get their hands on for Fisher's New York State property. The planting around the swimming pool is the most appealing horticultural experiment station imaginable. There, Fisher and Lyman test all manner of plants for aesthetic acceptability and garden adaptability, juxtaposing giant North American natives such as prairie dock, *Silphium terebinthinaceum,* with white lilies, familiar border plants, and extremely rare shrubs such as *Deutzia scabra* 'Variegata'. Fisher and Lyman have a discerning view and aesthetic priority that control their botanical cravings. The eclectic collection's astonishing achievement is, frankly, that it even exists. What is more remarkable is that it succeeds so beautifully.

Across the continent, Thomas Hobbs bought an eccentric 1920s Los Angeles–style house and created a garden with the feeling of the plants of that place and period. Only, his house and garden are in far-north Vancouver. His aesthetic style was dictated by the color and architecture of this unusual edifice. Plants that are not tropical but look it are here, along with the colors one would associate with the heyday of the movie industry capital. The look of Southern California imposes a rationale on Hobbs that directs his collector's zeal.

Although the aesthetes are influenced by appearance and design, they can identify with the hunters, missionaries, and spe-

ABOVE: *Thomas Hobbs selected plants that look tropical for his Los Angeles–style house in Vancouver.* FOLLOWING PAGES, CLOCKWISE FROM TOP LEFT: *Michael Schultz uses plants to express his garden fantasies. Huge leaves of* Gunnera manicata *accentuate the spaces that lead to a garden bench and a blue garden with gazing globes;* Clematis *and* Rodgersia pinnata *'Superba' echo reds by a birdbath;* Gunnera *peaks out over the gold* Filipendula ulmaria *'Aurea' that complements blue* Campanula portenschlagiana *flowers.*

ABOVE: *Ryan Gainey always places plants in his Georgia garden to express an aesthetic idea. Often understated, the colors and textures enhance the sculptural vignettes he creates with* Hedera canariensis 'Variegata' *in a window box,* LEFT; *textural evergreens,* CENTER; *and even humble plumes of* Asparagus densiflorus 'Meyers', RIGHT. *Robin Norris and Barbara Brockbrader grow ornamental edibles in colorful plantings,* BELOW, *such as a variegated corn,* Zea mays 'Gigantea Quadricolor', *in front of the tall purple grain* Amaranthus hypocondriacus. OPPOSITE: *A section of Barbara Flynn's garden has been devoted to plants with white in their foliage or flowers.*

cialists, too. Habitat aesthete collectors might gather interrelational plants from a certain place, Japan, for instance; but they are not the kinds of garden artists who make Japanese gardens. An authentic Japanese garden might have as few as a dozen kinds of plants—and that would never do for a collector. Collecting is still primarily about the passion for possessing plants—style comes second.

The aesthetes are adventurous collectors and many integrate sculpture into their schemes. There seems to be a common thread of eccentricity, too. Michael Schultz designed a garden for Geof Beasley and Jim Sampson south of Portland, Oregon. He became so involved in this project and in collecting plants for it that he moved to the property. The collaboration has led to the discovery and installation of plants to test his and the owners' artistic visions. A circular garden is filled with red-leafed plants—many of them quite rare. A Mexican watering can made from a colorful tin can may be both an accent for this garden and its inspiration.

Another place features plants with blue leaves and blue flowers, topped by blue gazing balls on stakes, and paving of smoothly polished shards of blue glass. A future design will be the nervous border, filled with discordant plants assembled to jar the viewer. This is a serious collection, made into a serious garden, but all with a great sense of whimsy.

In Decatur, Georgia, Ryan Gainey has created a world-famous garden. In spring, it appears quite traditional, except for Gainey's decidedly unconventional trappings. Here and there, you'll find cast-off iron for trellises, and urns on pillars built of overturned terra-cotta pots. A polychrome Portuguese jardinière forms the focal point of a round planting bed with radiating slabs of concrete pavers arranged like sunflower petals. These are evident when the foliage is sparse. However, it is in late summer and autumn when the true, shaggy nature of this place is revealed.

Gainey is a collector, and the plants he chooses have a decadent, fecund character that captures the faded glory of the Antebellum South. Shroudlike leaves of *Tetrapanax papyriferus* (rice-paper plants) drape over walls. The blowsy roses are in their final flush—pushing flowers through a broken wooden chair, dropping petals on the crazy paving. *Araujia sericifera* (cruel vine), a milkweed relative whose flowers snare flies, dangles plump gray-green pods from tendrils swagged over a rough-hewn pergola.

Garden designer Edith Eddleman of Raleigh, North Carolina, is known for her affinity for big plants. She is famous for two gardens; one, a public planting, features these giants, but the other, her home garden, focuses on small plants. This place is also shared by funky found objects—art—folk to fine. Many of the plants have tiny flowers. There is a large collection of miniature bulbs, for example, inspired by her idol, the late Elizabeth Lawrence, who wrote *The Little Bulbs: A Tale of Two Gardens* (1957). Gazing globes reflect scenes of the garden and enameled copper fish swim by. Children's toys bob on metal stakes. Wooden columns are topped by counterfeit stone finials made from galvanized chimney vents.

The enormous perennial border she designed at North Carolina State University Arboretum celebrates another scale altogether. In 1982, J. C. Raulston (page 63) dared Eddleman to design a planting. Part of the challenge was going to be her salary—$12.50 a week. Critics said, "You can't make a Jekyllesque border in the South" and "The age of the grand border is past." Saying "it can't be done" to Eddleman is a call to action. Today, a 250-foot-long border of grasses, tall prairie plants, and other big, bold, and beautiful plants thrives there.

The temper and the temperament of the aesthete collectors is evident in their creations. Charles Cresson's garden (pages 191–95) is somewhat like a museum; Wave Hill (pages 209–15) is a mecca for collectors who want to refine their art; Marcia Donahue's garden (pages 203–207) is a circus extravaganza. The personalities of the collectors behind these gardens are lavishly expressed. It is a joy to visit and share the vision of these people.

The aesthetes put it all together—color, texture, line, form—always with a conscious or subconscious awareness of the senses. They are the ultimate collectors—combining aspects of all the others and making the aesthetic use of plants their ultimate criterion.

Second Glances

It is a little annoying when you have a quarter acre of magnificent specimens and visitors dash by your prizes to drool over a single red hybrid tea rose that you were thinking of yanking out. Collectors are much more discerning. Sometimes they spend an hour in the garden, only to realize they have progressed just five feet.

Here is a small sampling of things that might be seen at second glance—examples of reasons to collect plants that go beyond flowers and the other first impressions of the garden.

OPPOSITE, CLOCKWISE FROM FAR LEFT: *Prehistoric* Equisetum hyemale *(horsetail) is exquisite but very invasive and should be contained in a pot; remember seeds for their ornamental attributes, such as woad* (Isatis tinctoria) *in front of silver Scotch thistle* (Onopordum acanthium); *one of the longest-cultivated plants, Job's tears* (Coix lacryma-jobi), *is a grass grown for seeds once used as beads; the bark of the cherry* Prunus serrula. RIGHT, TOP TO BOTTOM: *Oriental poppy petals last a few days, but their glaucus blue pods persist; the fruits of the female Osage orange tree; giant* Allium christophii *is a bit overwhelming in flower, but delicate, if extraterrestrial, in seed.*

Perhaps it might be a good idea to send a beginning collector outside to the garden with a magnifying glass, because when you begin to see plants close up, you find—in a leaf, in the bark of a tree, seeds, fruit, pods, and manners of growth—a world that until then was only known to nature.

OPPOSITE, CLOCKWISE FROM TOP LEFT: *The cones of* spruce (Abies *sp.*); *silver color from the seed pods of* Fibigia clypeata *reprised by* Elymus glaucus *and mediated by cerise* Epilobium dodonaei *flowers; 1 ½-inch-long fruits of Celandine poppy* (Stylophorum diphyllum) *dangle like earrings; translucent golden scales of a* Centaurea cuneifolia *ssp.* pallida *flower bud; the fruit of a species peony; fall's flowering kale* (Brassica oleracea)— *leaves as striking as flowers.*
RIGHT, TOP TO BOTTOM: Pulsatilla vulgaris *in mid-spring; followed by sparkling, feathery seedheads; the 5-inch-wide royal purple flowerheads of* Angelica gigas *in bud. The seeds of this one may self-sow and spread, so dead-head it after bloom.*

Although Jerry Flintoff is not a professional plantsman, he is the plant guru of the Seattle area. The breadth of his knowledge astounds northwestern gardeners, professional and amateur alike, and they make pilgrimages to share his wisdom. Many plants that enter the ornamental horticultural trade pass through his tiny suburban garden on their way to fame and fortune. This is where they make their debut and face a jury of their botanical peers, inferiors, or, if they prove unworthy of a permanent home, betters. The breadth of his collection is overwhelming.

To meet Flintoff, you would never imagine him to be a trendsetter. He is unassuming, reticent, and extremely private. But he inspires some of the most influential disseminators of information, taste, style, design, and plants in the country, and he has introduced several *Pulmonaria* varieties, including 'Roy Davidson' (named for a local plantsman) and 'Benediction' (named for Loie Benedict, a gardener from Auburn, Washington).

His entire collection, numbering thousands, resides on about $\frac{1}{5}$ acre surrounding a ranch house. There is no lawn or driveway—or rather, they were long ago covered by plantings and plants in pots, tubs, and flats. Great attention is paid to how these plants look with each other; in such close quarters, which grows next to what is important if the garden is to be more than a lineup.

187

OPPOSITE: *Vines grow up the front yard fence in a swirl from golden hop vine* (Humulus lupulus *'Aureus'*), *a Jackman-type* Clematis, *and the pewter leaves of* Vitis vinifera *'Purpurea', which glow garnet in autumn.* ABOVE: *The theme of plants arranged for romantic effect is continued in the garden behind the house, where roses spill over the fence to mingle with vivid rarities.*

There is the sense of an experiment station, too. The former driveway has been narrowed to a path by containers on one side and a remarkable assemblage of permanent plants on the other. The path leads to a shade house that may have been a carport in a past life. To the left, a collection of vines reveals in a small way what lies ahead: a Jackman-type clematis with a golden hop vine (*Humulus lupulus* 'Aureus') climbing through it, brilliantly sparking the purple clematis with a shock of chartreuse. Mediating this clash is the pewter- and red-wine-colored foliage of *Vitis vinifera* 'Purpurea', an ornamental grapevine.

The formal entrance to the rear garden is an English-cottage-style gate festooned with *Rosa* 'Ballerina', and roses dominate the view through the gate, as well. Huge shrub roses and climbers cover the fence forming the background for the plantings within. One that spills over is the collector's favorite rambler, 'Veilchenblau', whose abundant clusters of violet flowers fade to a wonderful earthy mauve and smell of green apples.

Every conceivable category of plants is here. A few are familiar, or, to be more precise, seem familiar. There are tree peonies, only they are 7 feet tall. A double-file viburnum is different, too—an unnamed selection with copper-colored foliage, not the usual dark green.

One foxglove here is very unlike its familiar cousins. *Digitalis parviflora* is shorter and the dense flowers are in shades of brown. Flintoff grows this strange species from the mountains of Spain as a drift of pointed floral racemes running along one side of the path that winds through the garden, itself, and then jumping across it to the other. The shades—copper, bronze, chestnut, and mahogany—are nearly beyond description, like Flintoff's garden itself, which might have the most concentrated collection of botanicals anywhere.

188

ABOVE: *The plants that line the path illustrate Jerry Flintoff's ebullient use of yellow-green and fawn-brown colors.* OPPOSITE, CLOCKWISE FROM TOP LEFT: *The tawny color of* Digitalis parviflora; *remarkable leaves and pale yellow flowers of* Disporum smithii *'Rick'; the tall spike of* Verbascum olympicum *provides an architectural note; feathery* Aruncus dioicus *'Kneiffii' blooms in front of an unnamed* Viburnum plicatum tomentosum *variety with bronze leaves and fruit.*

Charles Cresson collects nearly every intriguing, novel, or just plain beautiful plant that might fit into his Pennsylvania garden near Philadelphia. Flower form, foliage texture, bark color, growth structure—the plants' appearance is paramount. For in this place, design rules. His mission is to preserve and enhance the garden started by his grandfather in the 1920s. The property was purchased as a "gentleman's farm" by his great-grandfather in 1883, and named Hedgeleigh for the Osage orange hedges planted to enclose livestock. In 1909, a home was built down by the farm's old springhouse, and the name became Hedgeleigh Spring.

The buildings remain, along with old trees and a meandering stream that cuts through a meadow planted with crocus and daffodils in spring, and blooming with *Eupatorium purpureum, Silphium perfoliatum,* and *Helianthus giganteus* in summer. Grandfather William J. Cresson began a garden here on the two acres that are all that remain of the farm, which is now part of a suburban neighborhood. Charles Cresson has installed in the garden many rare plants and some of the best cultivars of given species that exist anywhere. Attached to his property both by birth and hard work, he spends every moment he can in the garden, even on occasion working into the night with a lighted miner's hat.

OPPOSITE: *The pool garden is much as it has been for three generations, but elaborated by Charles Cresson with purple Japanese iris and, in the water,* Iris laevigata *'Variegata'.* ABOVE RIGHT: *The fruit of the rare Western skunk cabbage* (Lysichiton americanum). ABOVE LEFT: *Near the pool,* Astilbe × thunbergii *'Ostrich Plume' blossoms with* Rodgersia sambucifolia. *Flowers are sparkling accessories to bold foliage arrangements.*

Professionals and local enthusiasts turn to him for erudite cultural information (especially on bulbs) and often for antique or scarce plants. For instance, there is a polyantha rose, 'Edith Cavell', still growing from the days of his grandfather, which was thought to be lost from cultivation until Charles identified it. Other examples are the native Western skunk cabbage, *Lysichiton americanum*, and its Japanese counterpart, *L. camtschatcencis*. Siskiyou Rare Plant Nursery in Medford, Oregon, gets seeds for these plants from Cresson. He may be the only gardener in the East to successfully grow the towering monocarpic lily, *Cardiocrinum giganteum*, which dies after it blooms—seven years from sowing.

How does a confirmed collector restrain from blurring a venerable garden's design? "I think the reason that my garden is not just a collector's garden is that any specimen has to have the right place to be allowed into the scheme," says Cresson. "I have a very strong point of view—convictions or criteria, if you will. A plant not only has to fit its location horticulturally. It has to fit the theme of the site visually: the background, be it stone or shade." Sometimes, something has to go in order to make room for an even more desirable addition. "The plant speaks to me and dictates a certain kind of environment. The palette of plants is limited to a certain spot. I won't stick it in the wrong place. If I get a new plant and I don't have that kind of space, I just won't have it. That becomes my limitation—it keeps me from violating the design."

ABOVE: *Unlike most fall-blooming toad lilies,* Tricyrtis latifolia, LEFT, *blooms in summer. A thornless raspberry shrub,* Rubus odoratus, *has fragrant 2-inch flowers,* RIGHT. OPPOSITE, CLOCKWISE FROM TOP LEFT: *Vines such as well-behaved coral* Lonicera sempervirens, *yellow* L. s. *'Sulphurea', and blue* Clematis alpina *grow on the back of the garage wall beyond a serendipitous bicolor poppy. A potted study in silver sits atop the gate post across from the garage; the path through the woodland garden;* Cardiocrinum giganteum *blooms there. This Brobdingnagian lily was Gertrude Jekyll's favorite, and Cresson was the first to grow it in the Northeast.*

A remarkable new fern would go into the fern dell along with pulmonarias. Hydrangeas—lace-cap *Hydrangea serrata,* double-flowered oakleaf *H. quercifolia* 'Snowflake', and others—flank either side of the path through this area. *Asarum,* of which there are many species, line the woodland walk. Succulents and cacti might find an unusual residence—the roof atop the little front porch.

Cresson is the author of several books and has become a mentor for novices whose interest takes them beyond the commonplace. His wisdom comes from years of experience, from his late grandfather, his father who now shares this life's work, and from his brother, Richard. Hedgeleigh Spring is a third-generation garden where the passion to collect merges with the mandate to preserve.

ABOVE, CLOCKWISE FROM TOP LEFT: *The U-shaped sunken garden is bordered by a white picket fence—made from recycled plastic lumber by brother Richard; the trellis garden includes varieties collected by Cresson's grandfather; a Martagon lily blooms by the back door; the front porch roof supports a hardy succulent garden.* OPPOSITE: *The flower garden with yellow violas, fuzzy lamb's ears, white astilbe, and foxgloves.*

A GENTEEL GARDENER WITH
A FLAMBOYANT EYE

What drives Nancy Goodwin's passion to collect? "Curiosity," she says, "... then anticipation. Nothing can match the thrill of seeing the first bud and then flower on a plant you've grown from seed for the first time. I don't think there's a cure. I cannot not garden, and I cannot not want to try new plants."

Curiosity drove Goodwin to grow the hardy *Cyclamen,* for which she is known throughout the country (see page 65). However, her extensive gardens—the more daring ones designed with collaborator Doug Ruhren—allude to other interests. When asked what her favorite plants are besides *Cyclamen,* she is nearly unable to answer: the thousands of species and varieties speed through her mind and register on her face as if an overloaded computer was about to crash.

But there is a theme to the plant selection besides the new, rare, and the beautiful. It is heat tolerance. She and her husband, Crauford, moved to Hillsborough, North Carolina, in 1977, after a ten-year search for just the right property. "I knew that I was going to be here for the rest of my life, so we searched in this area because it has the best soil. The challenge is to find plants that can tolerate

197

OPPOSITE: *A view of the new blue garden looking toward the barn,* ABOVE, *and the reverse view of the same area,* BELOW, *with tall* Aster tartaricus *in the foreground and the lathe house in the background.* ABOVE LEFT: *The transitional edge of the meadow with silver-leafed* Centaurea gymnocarpa *and white-flowered* Salvia farinacea *'Alba'.* ABOVE RIGHT: *An astounding planting of a gold* Coleus *whose name has been forgotten and tall castor bean (*Ricinus communis*).*

A
E
S
T
H
E
T
E
S

our summers," says Goodwin. "We have three other wonderful seasons, but there's always high humidity, warm nights, no breeze, and a drought in summer. We lose a lot, but we can grow a lot, too."

She is constantly adding new plants to the gardens, and new gardens to the property—especially since she closed Montrose, the mail-order nursery that for a decade kept her from devoting all the time she wanted to gardening. The gardens are driven by Goodwin's desire to try everything she possibly can. Sometimes she'll grow a plant to fill a need for color in one spot, texture in another, or just to test it out. "I'll kill it three times," she explains, as the general operating principle.

The wonderfully long autumn—an asset just beginning to be discovered by gardeners—spurred Goodwin's early collections of *Ilex* (holly) and *Viburnum,* and also of *Cyclamen* species, most of which are completely dormant in summer.

The gardens are planned for different seasons, and one of Goodwin's boundless special interests is bulbs. Here, again, autumn is celebrated, this time in a long border of *Colchicum* cultivars (autumn crocus) and fall-flowering *Crocus* subspecies in rockeries under the trees.

ABOVE: Setcreasea pallida *'Purple Heart' spills onto the path by the meadow garden.* OPPOSITE: *Two views of the gravel garden—toward the entrance arch,* ABOVE, *and the lathe house arch,* BELOW. *Hot-colored annuals include magenta* Petunia integrifolia, *small orange* Zinnia linearus, *large orange* Cosmos sulphureus, *red globe amaranth* (Gomphrena haageana *'Strawberry Fields'), tall red-orange Mexican sunflower* (Tithonia rotundifolia), *and red-leaved cannas.*

Goodwin has also been a champion of the renewed crusade to grow more unprocessed annuals: old-fashioned, prehybridized species, and tender perennials from the tropics and subtropics. Ruhren's obsession and talent for combining colors of flowers, leaf shape, texture, and scale are important assets in expanding the annual collection. He starts many from seeds from commercial English sources and from friends, and also takes hundreds of cuttings from this year's tender perennial winners, such as the numerous *Coleus* and *Salvia* varieties.

Most of the plantings are in full sun, but there is a shaded woodland garden with many *Cyclamen*, *Helleborus*, and *Rhodea japonica* cultivars. *Rhodea* is among the most popular plants in Japan, like *Hosta* here. There are hundreds of named varieties of this genus that is beginning to be feverishly collected by southern and northwestern connoisseurs.

Goodwin describes herself as a "rabid collector." But she is a collector with a conscience, and many plants, such as some of the ornamental grasses, are being weeded out because of their tendency to become invasive. "Even though they look so beautiful in the fall and winter, the *Miscanthus* is sowing everywhere. But I still have to try everything …"

OPPOSITE: *More views of the gravel garden show the purple thistlelike balls of* Gomphrena *and ornamental grasses, the annual purple grass* Pennisetum setaceum *'Rubrum', and* Miscanthus sinensis *'Gracillimus',* ABOVE. *Black sweet potato vine (*Ipomoea batatus *'Blackie') is the dominant ground cover,* BELOW. ABOVE: *Goodwin and Ruhren have collected annuals for the South's second gardening season—the long, luscious autumn when plants such as tall red castor bean and deep purple coleus thrive.*

Marcia Donahue's garden surrounding a Victorian house in Berkeley, California, is the product of an unblushing artist who is an omnivorous collector. "I want everything," she says, and simply embraces every bizarre oddity she meets. It's dangerous to shop with her, but worth it just to be in her illustrious company—and besides, you are likely to be given any extra plants.

"I have garden mania to an advanced degree," she has written of her obsession. "Sometimes when I'm out in the garden, or someone else's garden, I have the feeling of the skin being peeled away from my eyes. It's as if I'm seeing something for the first time, really seeing it. It's a feeling of a whole moment that just comes and fills me and buzzes me."

She is an exceptional artist collector and a model for us all, because her botanical knowledge and thirst for information is as great as her appetite for plants. She wants to know everything about them, not only their names but their families and kin. This aesthete is a professional sculptor whose famous carved heads appear in many of the collector's gardens in this book. Every Sunday, her house and garden, begun in 1981, are open to the public. "I knew back then if I got involved with this backyard, there would go the studio work, but I did, and I was right," she says. "But it's been worth it."

This place is a fantastic Eden—filled with nearly as much sculpture by her and her companion, Mark Bulwinkle, as with plants. Dragonflies light on the contorted form of the hardy trifoliate orange *Poncirus trifoliata* 'Flying Dragon'. Three cypresses, pruned by Donahue into spiraled totem poles, are the garden's only formal elements. She arranges plants completely for their aesthetic value.

203

OPPOSITE: *Nestled beneath a tree fern* (Dicksonia antarctica) *are voodoo lilies with palmate leaves* (Dracunculus vulgaris), *lance-leafed* Alpina zerumbet, *red-flowered* Abutilon, *and golden* Hakonechloa macra *'Aureola'. Donahue's bowling ball mulch and crockery art abound.* ABOVE, LEFT TO RIGHT: *Maroon* Dianthus *with a yellow bromeliad* Aechmea triangularis; *the artist's sculpted heads in serpentine stone with wiry* Corokia cotoneaster; *optical illusionist* Xanthorrhoea quadragulata.

The texture and color of leaves and the architecture of plant growth are paramount. *Chondropetalum tectorum*, a rarely used plant is the dryland version of *Equisetum*, the familiar wetland horsetail. Thin tubes rise out of the ground with stems and leaf-sheaths in green and buff pink. *Xanthorrhoea quadragulata* (Australian tall grass) forms spiny three-foot-tall spheres by the pool, the garden's central feature. She even has an area in which plants have been arranged for the appearance of their pubescent growth, what Donahue refers to as "organ meat plants," such as a form of *Rhododendron nuttallii*, which pushes wrinkled mauve leaves in spring. Her avant-garde use of plants is nonpareil.

Broken gravestones from the dump were recycled into a path that leads appropriately to the compost heap, and Donahue has become famous for her bowling ball mulch. "I've been collecting bowling balls for a long time—people just throw them out," she says. Colorful examples with swirled metallic hues mound in areas of the garden and are complemented by similarly toned plants. Broken blown-glass goblets are the flowers in one garden, and a ground cover of fork tines protects a special plant in a container.

"If something appeals, it's me. That's what tastes are, things that ring true to me. I'm not interested in the issue of good taste. By paying attention to what appeals to me, I'm trying to find out what I like and what I'm like."

PRECEDING PAGES, LEFT TO RIGHT: Elegeia capensis, Phormium cookianum *'Tricolor', and* Brahea armata.
ABOVE LEFT: *Marcia Donahue's spiral-pruned spires of* Cupressus sempervirens *'Skyrocket'.* ABOVE RIGHT: *Gazing globe sculpture by garden artist Simple, and metal springs by Mark Bulwinkle.* OPPOSITE: *A Donahue cairn replete with bowling ball is inscribed, "Cairn: Right Path."*

I've never thought of myself as a collector," says Marco Polo Stufano, Director of Horticulture at Wave Hill in the Bronx, New York, "not the way Harold Epstein (pages 29–31) is with Japanese plants or someone with a thousand hostas." He doesn't collect plants the way the specialists do. "I collect plants to add to the palette. I want to add as much as possible to the range of colors, textures, shapes, and seasons. This is a public garden, and it is my job to get people looking—it is all about seeing the plants, and seeing the world through plants. I hope Wave Hill raises people's awareness."

These are perfect thoughts for a collector whose prime directive is sharing the aesthetic quality of gardens and plants. Stufano trained as an art historian, and his approach to everything is through the senses. "I enjoy the world from an artist's view," he says. "I want objects around me that are beautifully made. Plants are beautifully made."

He is not only a passionate plant fiend, but a serious collector of high-style late-nineteenth-century furniture and ceramics, as well, a period of decorative arts that has had a major influence on his plant-

OPPOSITE: *The Palisades in New Jersey form the ultimate backdrop for the flower garden, where familiar plants (white-flowered* Hosta plantaginea *'Grandiflora') mingle with unusual tender perennials—pink* Impatiens balfourinana *and* Dahlia *'Bishop of Llandaff' with scarlet flowers and burgundy foliage.* ABOVE: *The centerpiece features a seasonal display of potted specimens, such as variegated boxwoods* (Buxus sempervirens *'Elegantissima') and tall* Pachypodium lamerei.

ing schemes. "People think of Victorian-era design as gaudy, dark, and heavy, but the later Aesthetic Movement has a lightness and a refinement, even though the designs are incredibly intricate. There is a lot of elaboration and ornamentation, but it is controlled and in an ordered framework."

If the framework of a garden is ordered and controlled, then a collection of innumerable varieties will hang together—you can always add plants if the structure holds. The Aesthetic Movement also introduced floral motifs and patterns in new ways. "Think of sunflowers in design, or mistletoe. Think of William Morris fabrics and wallpapers; and the colors upon colors, the intricate layering—that's what we're trying to do with the gardens."

Visitors to Wave Hill first see a beautiful garden, then, layer by layer, begin to understand the complexity. Here, every effort is made to enhance seasonal interest from the first spring bulb to the last falling leaf to the berries, bark, and hellebore flowers of winter. "We don't want to wow people with the expected regimented seasons of riotous color, but to try to impact on their eyes and minds the infinite variety of nature…. If they know begonias, then we want to show them a few that might surprise them," he says. "If they think of gardens only in the spring, we want to show them fall. If they assume that tropicals only belong in a greenhouse, then we want to show them how they do outdoors

ABOVE: *One spring, the entrance to the palm house was decorated with containers of* Sisyrinchium striatum, *an iris relative with cream flowers. Pots of orange* Mimulus longiflorus *and pansies, including a black* Viola *hybrid, are under the spreading branches of* Aralia elata *'Variegata'.* OPPOSITE, CLOCKWISE FROM TOP LEFT: *Climbing rose, 'Mmme. Grégoire Staechelin'; in late winter, color is found in the palm house; the flower garden's most brilliant time is late summer to early autumn; in May, old-fashioned peonies and foxgloves bloom.*

in a New York summer. Collecting the most interesting plants is the way to get these points across."

The salvias are a great case in point. Stufano began collecting them in 1976. They have to be pruned back and brought in for the winter or carried over as cuttings, but they are worth the extra trouble. By the late summer and early fall, they are in full color, ranging from the soft-apricot *Salvia greggii* 'Sanisidro Moon', to ruby-red *S. vanhoutii,* to the wonderful azure of *S. guaranitica* 'Argentine Skies'. "I wish the nursery industry would think of these plants the way they do geraniums—as bedding plants," he says, "and produce them for the summer market."

In typical nonconformist fashion, Wave Hill's color show peaks in late summer to fall. But Stufano eschews the attention paid to color, speaking about plant form and leaf texture. Wave Hill offers plants with natural sculptural qualities—trees, for example—and artificial ones, such as topiary standards. Stufano waxes on about big leaves, small, red, yellow, silver, blue, hard, soft, dull, shiny, pointy, lacy, wavy, fragrant, feathered, smooth, rough. "We want to show them all!"

When asked about the next new plants, he mentions some seeds coming via the Hardy Plant Society from Tony Avent (pages 97–99), who got them in Moscow. One plant he covets grows

OPPOSITE: *The focal point of the informal wild garden is a mature cutleaf sumac* (Rhus typhinia *'Laciniata')—interesting in every season, even winter.* ABOVE: *At the end of the growing year, this plant dominates the scene with fiery orange tones above a sea of silver* Cerastium tomentosum. *Plants chosen for their showy seed heads, faded flowers, and autumn foliage, along with the last flowering plants such as purple* Salvia leucantha, *make this moment in the garden as exciting as all other times of year.*

213

A
E
S
T
H
E
T
E
S

at Wisley, the Royal Horticultural Society's garden. "It's from Mexico, *Amicia zygomeris*, a piece of living sculpture with dried-blood-colored flowers." He has been trying to get one since 1980.

"We love to throw in an oddball here and there," says Stufano. "Something unexpected that will wow the visitors." He mentions the exotic *Tacca nivium*, a white batflower. "Something like that slows people down, they can hardly believe their eyes, pleated leaves, long whiskerlike staminodia. It is as beautiful as jewelry." Once you see this flower, you will never forget it—like viewing a masterpiece or like Wave Hill itself, one of the greatest living works of art.

Marco Polo Stufano shows visitors the unexpected—common plants used in unusual ways and rare plants they can grow. ABOVE, CLOCKWISE FROM TOP LEFT: *Blue* Clematis integrifolia; *silver cardoon* (Cynara cardunculus) *in a sea of* Coleus 'India Frills'; *the mysterious bulb* Nectaroscordum siculum; *a window box for shade with* Fuchsia austromontana 'Autumnale', *coleus, and white-edged ivy* (Hedera helix 'Little Diamond'). OPPOSITE: *The Aquatic Garden in fall.*

Collector's Guide

SOME NOTES ON PROPAGATION

All collectors have to propagate to feed their passion. It is the most economical way to increase a collection, and often the only possible way to acquire certain rare specimens.

Unusual plants are not found at the nursery for a number of reasons. If the demand for a particular plant is not great enough, professional growers cannot devote nursery space to it. If a plant grows too slowly, growers will avoid it. In the case of miniature evergreens, for example, a nursery cannot easily sell to the general public a plant that can barely be seen. From the collector's point of view, a conifer that grows $\frac{1}{2}$ inch a year is sensational for the rock garden. The only way to get a plant such as this may be to sow seed yourself. And that will be good for your garden, because a seedling will remain in scale with the tiny alpine plants for a long time. Rare plants will not stay rare for long, especially if they are easy to grow and to propogate—as are many of the ones shown in this book.

Essentially, there are two kinds of propagation: sexual and asexual (also called vegetative). Plants that are reproduced sexually are grown from seeds that result from the fertilization of ovules by pollen. Asexual means of propagation are varied, but obviously do not result from a sexual union. Plants can be started from cuttings taken from the stems, roots, or leaves. Grafting one plant to another is also an asexual means. Layering—rooting a part of a plant while it is still attached to the parent—is another.

Components of propagation can also be ornamental elements. The mountain silverbell (Halesia monticola), OPPOSITE, *has lovely white or pinkish flowers in the spring followed by dangling dry fruits that are not considered noteworthy except to Rick Darke (pages 137–39). He collects plants for the way they look in the light of the morning and evening, when he and horticulturist Melinda Zoehrer leave for and return from work.*

Some people have an uncanny knack for this thrilling part of gardening, and of course on a professional level, the results are even more impressive. It is startling to imagine that many commercially sold herbaceous perennials are begun from sections of roots less than $\frac{1}{2}$ inch long; but they are, under the guiding hands of a talented propagator. (See the Suggested Reading List [page 243] for manuals on propagation.)

I start seeds in 2- to 3-inch-square pots filled nearly to the top with a commercial sphagnum peat–based sowing mix. Generally, I bury the seeds to a depth equal to their thickness. Next, I borrow a tip from the rock gardeners. I sprinkle grit over the medium of all but the finest seeds. Rock gardeners use a layer of ⅛-inch chips of marble or granite, for example. Ask rock-gardening friends to share their source, or you can find chicken grit in bags at an agricultural supply store. The grit keeps the seeds in the medium from being disturbed if they are watered from above. Also, many seedlings die from a group of fungal diseases collectively called damping-off. Grit creates a somewhat sterile surface, because it is inert, unlike soil rich in organic matter that supports fungi and bacteria. Everything looks clean and tidy as well; and the emerging seedlings show up clearly against the stone.

Cuttings need a medium that holds moisture and oxygen to root quickly and successfully. Close contact with the medium—even a little bit of irritation—seems to encourage roots to grow. Experienced gardeners usually use rooting hormones on the wounded ends of cuttings. The hormones come in liquid or powder form and in different grades, depending on how difficult the cuttings are to root. Some hormone preparations also contain a fungicide that deters rotting.

Professionals also often use a misting box. A very fine mist of water is turned on automatically with a thermostat or timer for short intervals. This keeps the air humid, the cuttings full of water—essential for rooting—and lowers temperatures in the summer or in a sunny greenhouse. Few of us have misting benches or propagation boxes, but tents of plastic can also keep humidity high. A loose piece of plastic drop cloth draped over a homemade wire frame works well.

Not every method of propagation works for every plant (or every gardener). When experimenting with a new method, root a few cuttings of a plant in the usual way, and select very similar cuttings to try by a new method. One of my more interesting experiments of this type led me to use willow water for rooting fig tree cuttings. Rooting edible figs in water seems to work best for me. I placed a few cuttings in plain water, and a few in water with some cuttings of curly willow, *Salix matsudana* 'Tortuosa'. (I think any willow would work.) The cuttings in the willow water rooted faster. Willows root very easily and seem to give off a chemical that encourages roots on other plants.

I used to favor perlite, white exploded volcanic rock, as my rooting medium for nearly all cuttings, then I changed to coarse builder's sand, but have now learned a new method. Louis Bauer, the Greenhouse Manager at Wave Hill (pages 209–15) in the Bronx, New York, showed me how Director of Horticulture Marco Polo Stufano prepares a propagation bed for most cuttings.

This method also uses coarse perlite, but it is spread in a tray, moistened, and with a clean block of wood or other such tool, tamped down, hard. When the cuttings are ready, a small hole is made for each one in the perlite bed, it is inserted, and the disturbed perlite around the base of the stem is pushed down hard again. The contact with the cutting is so secure that the cutting cannot easily be pulled out of the medium. Plants root two to three times faster in the tamped perlite.

Few gardeners, even avid collectors, have greenhouses to start seeds and cuttings, but nearly everyone can afford the room and the expense of a cold frame. The best frames are built with most of the potting area underground. A familiar homemade frame has a top made from a recycled window, pitched at an angle to shed water. The tall side can be hinged and faced north to allow southern sun into the frame. An inexpensive foldable temporary frame made of corrugated translucent plastic works well for both propagating and extending the season.

Seeds of plants that can take the cold—hardy ones or cold-season annuals—can be sown directly in pots or flats in the frame, and the cold frame can be used to harden off all seedlings too. Instead of adapting plants to the outdoors by moving pots in and out of the house until they adjust to the sun and wind, seedlings can be set into the frame two weeks before they are ready to plant in the garden. Raising and lowering the lid of the frame serves to adjust the temperature, and for the busiest gardener, a temperature-sensing device opens and closes the top automatically.

SEND IN THE CLONES

How do you make enough of a plant asexually to supply a market that hungers for thousands of identical plants at a time? The answer lies in micropropagation—a form of vegetative reproduction in which 100,000 identical plants called clones can be made at a time.

Tropical orchids are being produced this way now. Orchids are very difficult to reproduce from seed—if the subject can be found that ever sets seed. Orchid seeds are usually started in sterile media, such as heat-treated whole sphagnum moss, in flasks. The meristem propagation, or tissue-culture procedure, is similar, but a tiny piece of tissue from the meristem, or growing point, is taken from the plant for reproduction. Since the environment must be completely free of pathogens, this is a laboratory procedure. Very often the plant tissue is semisterilized in a solution such as 10 percent bleach for a few seconds—no longer, because then it would be killed along with any contaminants. The tissue samples are kept alive and rooted within sterile vials in the gelatinous cultural medium called agar until they are strong enough to be transplanted as viable young plants. The results can be much more attractive from a commercial standpoint; many more plants produced.

Variegated leaf color, such as in Dan Heims's (pages 83–85) outstanding *Pulmonaria* and *Heuchera* introductions, is a genetic trait rarely passed on by sexual propagation. To reproduce his showy plants, he began a breeding program for his company, Tera-Nova. In a sterile laboratory run by his partner, Ken Brown, thousands of plantlets are lined up in petri dishes, test tubes, and flasks on their way to wholesale growers and, ultimately, your local nursery.

ALL IN THE NAME

Taxonomists—and by this I mean botanical scientists—seem to love to mess with plant names. Now that plants can be identified right down to their chromosomes, many have turned out to be something other than they were thought to be. Just when you get proud of yourself for remembering the name of sweet autumn clematis, *Clematis paniculata*, it gets changed to *C. maximowicziana*; and there has been word that this plant may get another name change.

Perhaps the most disturbing recent alteration happened to what we called *Chrysanthemum*. There is a colloquial phrase describing the two types of taxonomists: "lumpers and splitters." The first tends to combine various plants into a single genus; the splitters like to bust up a genus. The genus *Chrysanthemum* has been broken into distinct genera. Some plants are still *Chrysanthemum*, but others are now known as *Leucanthemum* or *Tanacetum*, and the old-fashioned flowers you buy in the spring and fall in pots are now known as *Dendranthema*. Many gardeners are a little fed up with all these alterations and refuse to conform to the changes—to them, *mum's* the word.

There is method to what might seem a bit mad. In 1753, the Swedish naturalist Carl von Linné, or *Linnaeus* (he Latinized his own name), first set forth the binomial or two-word classification for plants and animals. The first name is the genus and the second one identifies the species. The genus name often comes from an ancient Greek or Latin reference, the name of a god, for example. The second name, the specific epithet, is often descriptive. *Nymphaea odorata,* the common waterlily, is fragrant. Sometimes the species is named after its discoverer or by someone for someone. It is correct to Latinize the person's name. Dr. Augustine Henry, the doctor employed by the Chinese as a customs officer, lent his name to many plants. You'll see *Lilium henryi,* or *Parthenocissus henryana,* or even *Rhododendron augustinii* as specific names for plants. You may think of these plants as Henry's lily, Henry's Boston ivy, or Dr. Augustine Henry's rhododendron.

The descriptive, adjectival words, ones such as *alba* for white, or *fragrans* for fragrant, are frequently translated for common names. *Salix alba* is white willow. I have always called *Osmanthus fragrans* sweet olive, but it is known as fragrant tea or tea olive, which brings up the use and uselessness of common names. These can be helpful in letting you know what a plant might be like, but also not of any value when trying to locate one. So many plants have multiple common names, and often these are regional as well. But a *Rosa* is a *Rosa* is a *Rosa* in Burma or Bermuda. Another benefit to learning the correct Latin name for a plant is that it really helps you understand it as an individual, and one of the stages of becoming a great collector or gardener is to know the plants as distinctive.

Alba sometimes appears as *albus* or *album. Alba* is the feminine form, *albus* is masculine, and *album* is neuter. The specific epithet must conform with the gender of the genus. This is even true when the word tells of the place of origin or if the plant is named after its discoverer. Japan might become *japonica* or *japonicum,* as in *Camellia japonica* and *Viburnum japonicum.* Jean-Pierre Armand David discovered the dove or handkerchief tree while a missionary in China for the French, and it was named after him not as *Davidii,* but as *Davidia involucrata* (page 23).

In theory, two names are enough to describe every plant in nature. A species is the smallest common denominator, a plant that is found in a group of its like kind that can reproduce among its neighbors and produce nearly exact replicas of itself. Generally, a species will not cross with other species in its genus. In the case of hybrids, often made with the help of humans, but not always, interspecies reproduction does occur. Hybrids are often denoted with a multiplication sign in their names, which shows that a cross between species has been executed. For example, the species hybrid *Daphne* $\times$ *burkwoodii* is a cross of *Daphne caucasica* with *D. cneorum* (*D. caucasica* $\times$ *D. cneorum*). A plant whose name is preceded by an $\times$ is an intergenus hybrid: $\times$ *Pardancanda norrisii,* hybrid candy lily. But sometimes, growers use shorthand and offer hybrids such as *Geranium* 'Johnson's Blue' with no hint of its parentage.

When there are slight but distinctive variations in a population or strain of a species that seems to exist somewhat independently, this may be called a subspecies (ssp. or subsp.), variety (var.), or rarely, form (forma or f.). That would lead to a name for a version of the primrose *Primula vulgaris* ssp. *sibthorpii,* or one of the better-known native lady slipper orchids, *Cypripedium calceolus* var. *pubescens.* The northern pitcher plant, *Sarracenia purpurea,* has many variants including one named *S. purpurea* ssp. *purpurea,* and *S. purpurea* ssp. *purpurea* forma *heterophylla.* When a desirable, natural variation occurs—bigger flowers, more compact growth, variegation, for instance—the plant may be selected and reproduced vegetatively to make more available to gardens. This is called a cultivated variety, or cultivar.

The International Code of Nomenclature for Cultivated Plants established guidelines in 1953 stating that cultivars are "distinguished from other members of the same species or interspecific hybrid cross by any combination of genetic traits that may be significant in relation to the purposes for which the plants are cultivated; usually derived from a single selection of one plant or a small group of plants; and propagated by means that maintain a high degree of genetic uniformity among its member individuals."

A cultivar gets its name in single quotes with a capital letter, is generally not Latinized but may be, and is never printed in italics: *Solidago sphacelata* 'Golden Fleece' and *Hosta plantaginea* 'Grandiflora', for example. The latter is an old cultivar name and a good one; it tells that the flowers are big. But the current thinking is that cultivar names should be fancy, more like goldenrod 'Golden Fleece', a wonderful low-growing mound with arching yellow tassels (page 49).

The once-popular style of naming a cultivar after a person is nearly completely out of fashion. But I'm sure Mark Viette of Andre Viette Nursery in Virginia is thrilled to have had a double pink primrose named for him: *Primula acaulis* 'Mark Viette' (page 57). As you start to learn new plant names, you'll see horticultural luminaries turning up over and over: Carl Peter Thunberg, Philipp Franz von Siebold, Professor Charles Sprague Sargent (pages 22–23), Dr. Augustine Henry (page 23), Sir William Jackson, Sir Joseph Dalton Hooker, and the Veitch family (page 22), for example.

The latest confusion in nomenclature results from the controversial trademark names. These are supposed to be listed after the cultivar name to identify registered trademarks of growers who introduce a patented plant. A trademarked name, limiting propagation to the registration holder, is only effective for seventeen years. After that, anyone can propagate and sell the plant. The nursery intentionally tries to make consumers think that the trademarked name is actually the cultivar name so that at the end of the run of the exclusive rights, the buyer will ask for a plant by its formerly trademarked name and, therefore, receive it from the original wholesale grower who copyrighted the made-up name. The classic case could be with the Meserve hybrid hollies (*Ilex* × *meserveae*). These plants are erroneously known by trademarked names such as China Girl (*Ilex* × *meservea* 'Mesog') and Blue Stallion (*Ilex* × *meserveae* 'Mesan')—often labeled *Ilex* 'China Girl' and *Ilex* 'Blue Stallion', perhaps attempting to confuse a trademarked name for an actual hybrid or cultivar designation.

For gardeners, descriptive cultivar names that reveal something about the plant—the color of its flowers and habit of growth (*Aster novae-angliae* 'Purple Dome', for instance)—are more helpful. But if we must pick from what's out there, I still prefer *Clematis texensis* 'Betty Corning' to *Salvia* 'Hotpants', no matter how descriptive this cultivar name might seem to some.

THE LANGUAGE OF COLOR

Very often, the second name of a plant species or a cultivar includes descriptive information on flower or foliage color. Your knowledge of words will come in handy: *purpurea* means purple, *rosea* means rose-colored, for example. Here are some of the common colorful epithets you may encounter.

Aeneus	Bronze, copper colored	*Argophylla*	Silver leafed
Aeruginosus	Verdigris	*Argophyllus*	Silver leafed
Alba, albo	White	*Argyraeus*	Silvery
Album, albus	White	*Atamasco*	Red streaked
Albifrons	White fronds	*Ater*	Coal black
Amethystinus	Violet colored	*Atomarius*	Speckled
Argentea	Silver	*Atropurpurea*	Dark purple

Atrorubens........................	Dark red	*Niveum*..........................	Snow (white)
Atrovirens........................	Dark green	*Pallida, pallidus*...............	Pale green
Aurea, aureum..................	Golden yellow	*Pardinus*..........................	Leopard spotted
Aureolus...........................	Golden	*Picta, pictum, pictus*..........	Painted
Bicolor...........................	Two toned	*Picturatus*........................	Variegated
Cadmicus........................	Metallic	*Purpurea, purpureum*........	Purple
Caesius...........................	Bluish gray	*Quadricolor*.....................	Four colored
Calophrys........................	Dark margined	*Reticulata*........................	Netted, veined
Candida, candidum..........	White	*Rosea, roseum, roseus*.........	Rose colored
Canus..............................	Ash colored	*Rubens*............................	Red colored
Chrysophyllus...................	Gold leafed	*Rubra, rubrum*..................	Red
Cineracus........................	Covered with gray hairs	*Rubricaulis*......................	Red stemmed
Coccinea..........................	Scarlet	*Rubronervos*.....................	Red veined
Colorata, coloratus...........	Colored	*Rufus*..............................	Red
Concolor..........................	Unvaried in color	*Rutifolius*.........................	Blue-gray foliage
Conspersus.......................	Speckled	*Sanguinea*........................	Blood red
Cyanophyllus...................	Blue leaved	*Sempervirens*....................	Evergreen
Dealbatus........................	White washed	*Striata, striatum*...............	Striped
Discolor...........................	Differently colored	*Sytriatus*..........................	Striped
Flava, flavum..................	Pale yellow	*Tessellatus*........................	Checkered
Galbinus..........................	Yellowish green	*Tricolor*...........................	Three colored
Glauca, glaucum...............	Blue gray	*Variegata, variegatum*........	Variegated
Guttatus..........................	Spotted	*Variegatus*........................	Variegated
Lacteus............................	Milk white	*Venosus*............................	Veiny
Laetesvirens......................	Bright green	*Versicolor*........................	Variably colored
Lividus............................	Lead colored	*Vinosus*............................	Wine red
Luridus............................	Pale yellow	*Virens*..............................	Green
Lutea, luteum...................	Yellow	*Virescens*..........................	Light green
Maculata, maculatum........	Splotched, spotted	*Viridifolius*......................	Green leaved
Marginata, marginatum....	Margined	*Viridis*.............................	Green
Meleagris.........................	Speckled	*Xanthacanthus*.................	Yellow spined
Mesoleucus.......................	White center	*Xanthophyllus*.................	Yellow leaved
Mosaicus.........................	Colored like a mosaic	*Zebrinus*..........................	Zebra striped
Multicoloris.....................	Multicolored	*Zonalis, zonatus*...............	Zoned, banded

MAIL-ORDER NURSERIES

Mail-order nurseries are the most accessible sources for unusual plants. These businesses are most often labors of love by individuals, couples, or families, who have turned every square inch of their property over to plants. We have to do all we can to help keep these wonderful people. Therefore, a few points of mail-order etiquette are worth mentioning. If money or postage is requested for a catalog or list, send it—very often the amount is deductible or refundable from the first order. Always call or write before attempting to visit a nursery, since many are not set up for this, but may take you by appointment, or may have specific days and hours for visits. Lastly, be sensitive about when you call; odds are that unless the catalog has a number for taking orders, you will be reaching a private phone line. Be sensitive to proprietors' needs; they will appreciate it and will be more happy to have you come. This said, a visit to a nursery can be a thrilling experience.

Should you find yourself on a trip to an area rich in nurseries, gardens, and arboreta, such as Chapel Hill, North Carolina, arrange in advance to visit some nurseries as well as the public gardens.

Some of the best mail-order nurseries are listed in the source guide. A few of the most interesting new and long-established rare-plants companies with which I have dealt personally are described below. Nurseries persevere, such as Greer Gardens, in Eugene, Oregon, and Gossler Farms, in Springfield, Oregon. The Gossler family has had a retail mail-order business for over a quarter-century. Today, son Roger heads the operation. The nursery started in 1962 as part of the Gosslers' farm along with crops of sweet corn and peppermint. In 1968, the first mail-order catalog was printed. The farm continued until the mail-order business became full time. Today, they specialize in magnolias, but offer many other woody plants. The extensive garden with over 4,000 varieties is open to the public by appointment. Gossler's criteria for listing plants is: "the plant must be beautiful for at least one season (flowers, fruits, stems); it isn't available from everyone else; the plant is reasonably easy to grow without dousing with pesticides, etc.; last, but not least, it has to attract our eye and we enjoy growing the plant in our garden." The only complaint I've heard is that they offer different plants each year. Aficionados who are desperate for a particular plant and hear that the source is Gossler may discover that it isn't in the current catalog because "Roger Gossler is into something new."

Greer Gardens is nearly as old as Gossler Farms. Greer, too, is open to visitors, year round. As Harold Greer says, "there is always something to see even in winter." This rare-plant nursery specializes in deciduous and evergreen *Rhododendron*, but is one of the best sources for other unusual flowering and evergreen woody plants, as well. Its first catalog in 1969 was three pages; in 1994, it was 144.

Most *Rhododendron* species or hybrids are for sale here. The plants are well grown and of good size, and service is excellent. Once I called about a specific woody plant (*Robinia pseudoacacia* 'Frisia'), and someone went out into the nursery to check on the size and condition of the plant. If you are looking for a matched pair of a certain rare dwarf evergreen, for example, you might be able to request this, although you'd be wise to avoid the springtime rush for such special orders.

Another venerable source is Louisiana Nursery, started in 1950, which sells "Magnolias and other Garden Aristocrats." Louisiana actually offers more than 400 magnolias, 75 camellias, and about 175 hollies, and it also prints specialty catalogs on other plants, such as Louisiana iris, which are filled with information that might be available only here. Louisiana has plants that no one else does, but the prices are high. This is the only nursery I know of that offers *Schisandra chinensis* (magnolia vine), for example, a wonderful climber that bears elegant white flowers and hanging, grapelike clusters of red fruits—in shade. This plant is easy to propagate, but fetches a high price for its rarity in the trade. But then again, this is a nursery offering literally thousands of shrubs and trees, including sixteen *Hydrangea quercifolia* (oak-leaf hydrangea) cultivars—remarkable!

Another woody plant purveyor, Roslyn Nursery, came into being in part through Nick Nickou (pages 39–41), a hunter-collector whose own finds have been introduced to the trade through the efforts of his friend Phil Waldman. Waldman collects at Nickou's for his Roslyn Nursery. "When Phil first came here fifteen years ago, he asked if he could take some cuttings—he seemed to know what he was doing," says Nickou. "He placed each cutting in a small plastic bag and then all of those bags in larger ones. By the time he was ready to go, he couldn't close the trunk of his car. He admitted at the end of that day that two years before, he didn't know a dahlia from a rhododendron." Today, Roslyn is famous for rare plants and woodies, including some of Nickou's *Rhododendron, Enkianthus,* and *Acer* selections.

Conifers are favorites of collectors and many nurseries offer them, including the young Collector's Nursery, which is a company to watch. Each year, these Northwesterners offer more and more unusual plants, and the proprietors, Bill Janssen and Diana Reeck, are two of the most helpful nursery owners in the business.

Rarifolia is also a new nursery, but it specializes exclusively in dwarf conifers and has a list of over 400. Robert Fincham, another Oregonian, has a personal collection numbering 2,000 dwarf conifers. His nursery, Coenosium Gardens, offers 600 cultivars.

Just about the greatest variety of woody plants, natives and exotics, can be found in Ray and Peg Prag's 350-page Forest Farm catalog, also from Oregon. Most of the offerings are young plants in small square paper tubes. For less-patient gardeners, however, a good percentage are also available in 1- and 5-gallon containers for reasonable prices, but the cost of shipping on these makes the purchase take more than a little deliberation. All of their plants are nursery propagated.

The comprehensive list is thrilling. A collector of redbud, a small spring-blooming native tree of the forest understory, for example, will have far more than the species to choose from. In addition to the pink-blossomed eastern redbud, *Cercis canadensis,* Forest Farm sells a white form (*C. canadensis* 'Alba'). There is also *C. canadensis* 'Flame' with double flowers; *C. canadensis* 'Forest Pansy' with rosy-purple leaves; the heat-resistant *C. canadensis* 'Oklahoma' with shiny leaves; *C. canadensis* 'Rubye Atkinson' with shell-pink flowers; and one species of the Chinese redbud, *C. chinensis.* The drought-tolerant Western native, *C. occidentalis,* is here, as is *C. reniformis* 'Alba', a white-flowered cultivar of the Texas redbud that has glossy, leathery leaves. Nearly all of these plants also have yellow fall foliage color.

Like the Pacific Northwest, the Southeast is home to many mail-order nurseries. Sunlight Gardens in Tennessee offers eastern North American native shrubs, ferns, and perennials, as does Niche Gardens in North Carolina. Holbrook Farm near Asheville, North Carolina, has a wonderful display garden that owner Alan Bush uses to house his stock plants for cuttings and seeds.

When I visited collector's gardens around the country, two nurseries were mentioned consistently as sources for some of the plants in nursery people's own gardens: Woodlanders in South Carolina and We-Du Nurseries in North Carolina. Woodlanders list 1,000 rare plants—native and exotic—including South Carolina endangered plants that can only be sold within that state. The purveyors are adamant about offering nursery-propagated stock only and not wild-collected material. We-Du has been an inspiration to many of the other suppliers of rare plants. Specializing in Southeastern natives and their analogous Asian counterparts, they appeal to a range of collectors. Many of the plants are excellent candidates for shady gardens.

The Sandy Mush Herb Nursery, in the Blue Ridge Mountains near Asheville, North Carolina, has a pretty garden, and is open to the public a few days a week. Call ahead—not just for hours, but detailed directions up the winding dirt roads and over sheer rock ledges. This is one of the best sources for the increasingly popular salvias (sages). They have nearly one hundred ornamental and culinary sages, offered as little rooted cuttings. Many people put their orders in early and expect to grow the plants on well into the late summer and fall, when so many bloom in northern zones.

More salvias can be found in the catalog from Canyon Creek Nursery, in Oroville, California—another one of the collector's secret sources. The sages are just some of the herbs and other hardy and tender perennials available from this California nursery.

Canyon Creek and Sandy Mush are good sources for colorful plants to grow as annuals. Perhaps the best source of all for tender plants is the 100-plus-year-old nursery Logee's Greenhouses, in Danielson, Connecticut. This is the place for begonias and scented geraniums—plants for which the owners, the Logee and Martin family, are renowned. But the nursery also presents incredible, tender flowering vines and shrubs—rare, unusual, and beautiful plants too numerous to name. It is also the source for tender plants for the window garden, greenhouse, annual planting, herb garden, and, most of all but often overlooked, for permanent plantings in the warm zones. Gardeners in California, Texas, Louisiana, and even the Southwest could look here. This is the best source for *Brugmansia*, for instance, and they also offer old-fashioned camellia and citrus varieties. One tip for a visit, which is a must: The plants you get through the mail from Logee's are often better individuals than the ones selected off the benches, and cheaper, too.

Glasshouse Works is another nursery offering hundreds of possible tender plants for seasonal color outside—with variegation as the thread that runs through many of the inclusions. This is mainly a greenhouse and houseplant company, but when you see the list of impatiens, coleus, fuchsia, and geraniums, your urns, window boxes, and outdoor summering houseplant collections will practically design themselves. Many of these plants can be carried over through the winter, but better still, propagate cuttings in the fall to grow indoors and plant out again in spring, and order more.

In the West, the similar source is Kartuz Greenhouses. Fewer of the plants offered by this nursery would be suitable to outdoor conditions, but their list of *Passiflora*, passionflower vine species and cultivars, for instance, is very large. Some of these are hardy to Zones 7 or lower.

Thompson and Morgan is a British seed company with a North American outlet that has the most unusual flowering and foliage, tender and hardy perennials and annuals. This is the source for such plants as *Mina lobata*, the unusual vine with flowers that change color from red to yellow to cream, so that there are many colors at a time; banana-plant seeds; our native annual, *Euphorbia marginata* (snow-on-the-mountain). There are exciting biennials, such as the *Campanula* relative *Michauxia tchihatcheffii* (*Mindium tchihatcheffii*), with 2-inch shooting-star-like flowers. There are also hardy and half-hardy perennials such as *Codonopsis clematidea*, with bell-like nodding pale-blue flowers; the brown-black columbine *Aquilegia viridiflora*; and the astonishing climbing blue monkshood, *Aconitum volubile*. The rarest seeds go quickly, so order as soon as the catalog comes.

J. L. Hudson, Seedsman, based in California, is the continuation of a business started in 1911. Hardy and tender trees, shrubs, herbaceous perennials, annuals, and vegetables squeeze into 95 pages jammed with descriptions. The catalog is not in color, but there are charming illustrations, and more important, very weird plants that you can't find anywhere else. Hudson's is a no-nonsense operation with clear-cut rules: "I have no business or personal telephone. Please do not call anyone named Hudson who is listed in the Redwood City Directory, as you will only disturb someone who is not connected with me. We are not set up to receive visitors."

Both seeds and plants are available from Plants of the Southwest, a company that I've had the pleasure to watch grow through their sophisticated catalog. There was a time when theirs was the only such business of its kind, and it is still one of the best sources for hot and dry climates. They have grasses and xerophytes, but also offer salvias and, even more exciting, penstemons—pages of them. They are also a source of Buffalo grass seed, *Buchloe dactyloides,* for lawn alternatives in the short-grass plains states.

Rocky Mountain Rare Plants (pages 161–63) sells seeds of alpine plants at very reasonable prices. Arrowhead Alpines also has an impressive seed list.

The best source for alpines and other dwarf, hardy plants for the woodland and rock garden is the Siskiyou Rare Plant Nursery. This nursery is not just an inspiration to collectors, it is a necessity. Baldassare Mineo, who began the nursery in the sixties, is spoken about by collectors as a friend and mentor, whether they have met him or not. All the rock gardeners in this book send plants or seeds to him, and all buy from him. The dwarf conifer list is impressive, as are the dwarf woodies, such as some of the alpine willows. There are many plants offered here that cannot be found in any other nursery.

Another area of specialty is water gardening. The leader in this very sophisticated field would have to be Lilypons; I recommend it as an example for the other companies that often have similar plants at competitive prices. In addition to water lilies, Lilypons offers other beautiful water plants, such as the lotus (*Nelumbo* species and cultivars) and hard-to-find bog and waterside plants, including natives and irises. The Lilypons catalog is not just a catalog: It is a resource nearly as good as any book on the subject. It includes instructions and illustrations on how to install a water garden and even has a chart of fish diseases and how to treat them. Reading it makes any gardener want to go out in January with a pickax to start digging up the frozen ground.

The Lilypons catalog is printed in full color, as are some of the others listed above—but most are not. Keep in mind that color has a price, often in the actual amount paid for younger or smaller plants. Some of the best companies have nothing more than a photocopied list, although, in general, the most reliable companies have something in between, usually a booklet with a few line drawings and wonderful description of plants.

The following list was prepared with the help of the Metro Hort Group, a New York City regional association of professionals in horticulture and related fields. Read the descriptions of nursery specialties and visit their Web sites. Try to order catalogs from those Web sites or via fax. Many mail-order sources charge a fee for catalogs and postage. These fees change frequently and have not been included in the list.

Please bear in mind that it is very hard for nurseries to chat during the peak shipping seasons, and since some of these operations are small, you may be calling someone's home. Do not call too early in the morning or at night. Check the time zones, as well.

Mail-order Sources for Collector's Plants

Amanda's Garden
8410 Harper's Ferry Road
Springwater, NY 14560
E-mail: efolts4826@aol.com
Telephone: 585-669-2275
Wildflowers and native perennials

Ambergate Gardens
8730 Country Road 43
Chaska, MN 55318-9358
E-mail: mjhamber@aol.com
Web site: www.ambergategardens.com
Telephone: 877-211-9769
Fax: 952-443-2248
Martagon lilies, bare-root perennials

Antique Rose Emporium
9300 Lueckmeyer Road
Brenham, TX 77833-6453
E-mail: roses@industryinet.com
Web site: www.weareroses.com
Telephone: 800-441-0002
Fax: 979-836-0928
*Antique, shrub, and climbing roses on their own
roots and in pots*

ArborVillage Nursery
P.O. Box 227
15806 Country Road "CC"
Holt, MO 64048
Web site: www.arborvillagellc.com
Telephone: 816-264-3911
Fax: 816-264-3760
Collector's trees and shrubs

Arena Rose Company
P.O. Box 3570
Paso Robles, CA 93447
Web site: www.arenaroses.com
Telephone: 888-466-7434
Bare-root roses

Arrowhead Alpines
P.O. Box 857
Fowlerville, MI 48836
Web site: www.arrowheadalpines.com
Telephone: 517-223-3581
Fax: 517-223-8750
Perennials, rock plants, and conifers

Arrowwood Nursery
870 W. Malaga Road
Williamstown, NJ 08094
E-mail: njplants@aol.com
Telephone: 856-697-6045
Fax: 856-697-6050
Native trees, shrubs, and perennials

Asiatica
P.O. Box 270
Lewisberry, PA 17339
E-mail: asiatica@nni.com
Web site: www.asiaticanursery.com
Telephone: 717-938-8677
Fax: 717-938-0771
*Arisaema, Asarum, and Asian woodland
plants*

David Austin Roses
15059 Highway 64 West
Tyler, TX 75704
E-mail: usa@davidaustinroses.com
Web site: www.davidaustinroses.com
Telephone: 800-328-8893
Fax: 903-526-1900
English and other shrub and climbing roses

Avant Gardens
710 High Hill Road
Dartmouth, MA 02747
E-mail: plants@avantgardensne.com
Web site: www.avantgardensne.com
Telephone: 508-998-8819
Fax: 866-442-8268
*Annuals, perennials, grasses, rock garden plants,
and woody plants*

Bach's Cactus Nursery
8602 N. Thornydale Road
Tucson, AZ 85742
Web site: www.bachs-cacti.com
Cacti and succulents

Baker Creek Heirloom Seeds
2278 Baker Creek Road
Mansfield, MO 65704
E-mail: seeds@rareseeds.com
Web site: www.rareseeds.com
Telephone: 417-924-8917
Fax: 417-924-8887
Heirloom seeds

Bamboo Sourcery
666 Wagnon Road
Sebastopol, CA 95472
E-mail: bamboosource@earthlink.net
Web site: www.bamboosourcery.com
Telephone: 707-823-5866
Fax: 707-829-8106
Bamboo plants and products

Banana Tree
715 Northampton Street
Easton, PA 18042
E-mail: info@banana-tree.com
Web site: www.banana-tree.com
Telephone: 610-253-9589
Fax: 610-253-4864
Tropical plants and seeds

Kurt Bluemel
2740 Greene Lane
Baldwin, MD 21013-9523
E-mail: bluemels@aol.com
Web site: www.kurtbluemel.com
Telephone: 800-498-1560
Grasses and perennials

Bluestone Perennials
7211 Middle Ridge Road
Madison, OH 44057-3096
E-mail: bluestone@
bluestoneperennials.com
Web site: www.bluestoneperennials.com
Telephone: 800-852-5243
Fax: 440-428-7198
Small, inexpensive perennial plants

Borbeleta Gardens
15980 Canby Avenue
Faribault, MN 55021
Telephone: 507-334-2807
Fax: 507-334-0365
Lilies, irises, daylilies, and peonies

Botanique
387 Pitcher Plant Lane
Stanardsville, VA 22973
E-mail: botanique@pitcherplant.com
Web site: www.pitcherplant.com
*Carnivorous plants, Calopogon orchids, and
native plants*

Bowman's Hill Wildflower Preserve
P.O. Box 685
New Hope, PA 18938-0685
E-mail: bhwp@bhwp.org
Web site: www.bhwp.org
Telephone: 215-862-2924
Fax: 215-862-1846
Wildflower seeds

Brent & Becky's Bulbs
7900 Daffodil Lane
Gloucester, VA 23061
E-mail:
info@brentandbeckysbulbs.com
Web site:
www.brentandbeckysbulbs.com
Telephone: 804-693-3966
Fax: 804-693-9436
Hardy and tender bulbs

Broken Arrow Nursery
13 Broken Arrow Road
Hamden, CT 06518
E-mail: brokenarrow@snet.net
Web site:
www.brokenarrownursery.com
Telephone: 203-288-1026
Fax: 203-287-1035
Kalmia, Rhododendron, *and woody plants*

David Burdick
P.O. Box 495
Dalton, MA 01227
E-mail: daffodil@berkshire.net
Telephone: 413-443-1581
Antique daffodils

W. Atlee Burpee & Co.
300 Park Avenue
Warminster, PA 18991-0001
Web site: www.burpee.com
Telephone: 800-888-1447
Seeds and plants

D. V. Burrell Seed Growers Co.
P.O. Box 150
405 N. Main
Rocky Ford, CO 81067-0150
E-mail: burrellseeds@rmi.net
Telephone: 719-254-3318
Fax: 719-254-3319
Seeds

Busse Gardens
17160 245th Avenue
Big Lake, MN 55309
E-mail: customer.service@
bussegardens.com
Web site: www.bussegardens.com
Telephone: 800-544-3192
Fax: 763-263-1473
Perennials and hostas

Caladium World
P.O. Box 629
Sebring, FL 33871-0629
Web site: www.caladium.com
Telephone: 863-385-7661
Fax: 863-385-5836
Caladium *tubers*

Camellia Forest Nursery
9701 Carrie Road
Chapel Hill, NC 27516
E-mail: info@camforest.com
Web site: www.camforest.com
Telephone: 919-968-0504
Fax: 919-960-7690
Camellias

Canyon Creek Nursery
3527 Dry Creek Road
Oroville, CA 95965
E-mail: johnccn@sunset.net
Web site: www.canyoncreeknursery.com
Telephone: 530-533-2166
Wonderful unusual perennials

Carino Nurseries
P.O. Box 538
Indiana, PA 15701
E-mail: info@carinonurseries.com
Web site: www.carinonurseries.com
Telephone: 724-463-3350
Fax: 724-463-3050
Seedlings and sapling trees

Carlson's Gardens
P.O. Box 305
26 Salem Hill Road
South Salem, NY 10590
E-mail: bob@carlsonsgardens.com
Web site: www.carlsonsgardens.com
Telephone: 914-763-5958
Rhododendrons

Carroll Gardens
444 E. Main Street
Westminster, MD 21157-5540
Web site: www.carrollgardens.com
Telephone: 800-638-6334
Fax: 410-857-4112
Fancy perennials

Chiltern Seeds
Bortree Stile
Ulverston, Cumbria, LA12 7PB
England
E-mail: info@chilternseeds.co.uk
Web site: www.chilternseeds.co.uk
Telephone: +44 (0) 1229 581 137
Fax: +44 (0) 1229 584 549
Hard-to-find seeds of rare plants

Cloud Mountain Farm
6906 Goodwin Road
Everson, WA 98247
E-mail: info@cloudmountainfarm.com
Web site:
www.cloudmountainfarm.com
Telephone: 360-966-5859
Fax: 360-966-0921
General plant catalog; fruit and nut trees

Cold Stream Farm
2030 Freesoil Road
Freesoil, MI 49411-9752
E-mail: csf@jackpine.com
Web site: www.jackpine.com/~csf/
Telephone: 231-464-5809
Trees and shrubs

Collector's Nursery
16804 N.E. 102nd Avenue
Battle Ground, WA 98604
E-mail: dianar@collectorsnursery.com
Web site: www.collectorsnursery.com
Telephone: 360-574-3832
Fax: 360-571-8540
Fabulous collector's plants

Color Farm
1604 W. Richway Drive
Albert Lea, MN 56007
E-mail: vjogren@charter.net
Web site: www.colorfarm.com
Telephone: 507-377-2572
Coleus

Colvos Creek Nursery
P.O. Box 1512
24029 59th Avenue S.W.
Vashon Island, WA 98070
Telephone: 206-749-9508
Fax: 206-749-0446
Drought-tolerant trees, shrubs, and perennials

Companion Plants
7247 N. Coolville Ridge Road
Athens, OH 45701
E-mail: complants@frognet.net
Web site: www.companionplants.com
Telephone: 740-592-4643
Fax: 740-593-3092
Annuals, perennials, seeds, and plants

Completely Clematis Specialty Nursery
217 Argilla Road
Ipswich, MA 01938-2617
E-mail: info@clematisnursery.com
Web site: www.clematisnursery.com
Telephone: 978-356-3197
Clematis

Comstock, Ferre & Co.
263 Main Street
Wethersfield, CT 06109
E-mail: comstock@tiac.net
Web site: www.comstockferre.com
Telephone: 800-733-3773
Fax: 860-571-6595
Seeds

Conard-Pyle Co.
372 Rose Hill Road
West Grove, PA 19390-0904
Web site: www.conard-pyle.com
Telephone: 610-869-2428
Fax: 610-869-0651
Roses and ornamental shrubs

Cook's Garden
P.O. Box 1889
Southampton, PA 18966-0859
E-mail: info@cooksgarden.com
Web site: www.cooksgarden.com
Telephone: 800-457-9703
Fax: 800-457-9705
Vegetable seeds

Cooley's Gardens
P.O. Box 126 NT
Silverton, OR 97381-0126
E-mail: cooleyiris@aol.com
Web site: www.cooleysgardens.com
Telephone: 503-873-5463
Fax: 503-873-5812
Irises

Cricket Hill Garden
670 Walnut Hill Road
Thomaston, CT 06787
Web site: www.treepeony.com
Telephone: 877-723-6642
Fax: 860-283-5508
Chinese tree peonies

The Crownsville Nursery
P.O. Box 309
Strasburg, VA 22657
E-mail:
questions@crownsvillenursery.com
Web site: www.crownsvillenursery.com
Telephone: 540-631-9411
Fax: 540-631-9414
General perennial nursery

The Cummins Garden
22 Robertsville Road
Marlboro, NJ 07746
Telephone: 732-536-2591
Native and non-native azaleas

Cummins Nursery
738 W. Hunt Road
Alcoa, TN 37701
Web site: www.cumminsnursery.com
Telephone: 865-681-8423
Fruit and nut trees

Dabney Herbs
P.O. Box 22061
Louisville, KY 40252
E-mail: dabneyherb@win.net
Web site: www.dabneyherbs.com
Telephone: 502-893-5198
Herbs

Dave's Nursery
234 Willow Avenue
Pompton Lakes, NJ 07442
E-mail: davesnursery@prodigy.net
Web site: www.davesnursery.com
Telephone: 973-839-6390
Fax: 973-831-7777
Conifers and maples

David Brothers Bean Road Nursery
P.O. Box 123
Worcester, PA 19490-0123
Web site: www.davidbrothers.com
Telephone: 610-584-1550
Fax: 610-584-8815
Native plants

Daylily World
P.O. Box 1612
Sandford, FL 32772-1612
E-mail: hybridizer@aol.com
Web site: www.daylilyworld.com
Telephone: 407-322-4034
Fax: 407-322-4026
Daylilies

Deer Resistant Landscape Nursery
3200 Sunstone Court
Clare, MI 48617-8600
E-mail: sales@deerxlandscape.com
Web site: www.deerresistantplants.com
Telephone: 800-595-3650
Fax: 888-727-3337
Deer-resistant plants

Digging Dog Nursery
P.O. Box 471
Albion, CA 95410
E-mail: business@diggingdog.com
Web site: www.diggingdog.com
Telephone: 707-937-1130
Fax: 707-937-2480
Cool perennials, grasses, callunas, ericas, trees, and shrubs

Jim Duggan Flower Nursery
1452 Sante Fe Drive
Encinitas, CA 92024
E-mail: jimsflowers@thebulbman.com
Web site: www.thebulbman.com
South African bulbs

Eartheart Gardens
1709 Harpswell Neck Road
South Harpswell, ME 04079
E-mail: earthart@gwi.net
Telephone: 207-833-6327
Fax: 207-833-6905
Japanese and Siberian irises

Eco-Gardens
P.O. Box 127
Decatur, GA 30031
Telephone: 404-294-6468
Southeastern natives and selections

Edmunds Roses
6235 S.W. Kahle Road
Wilsonville, OR 97070-9727
E-mail: info@edmundsroses.com
Web site: www.edmundsroses.com
Telephone: 888-481-7673
Fax: 503-682-1275
Roses

Elkhorn Native Plant Nursery
P.O. Box 270
Moss Landing, CA 95039
E-mail: enpn@elkhornnursery.com
Web site: www.elkhornnursery.com
Telephone: 831-763-1207
Fax: 831-763-1659
Native plants

Ensata Gardens
9823 E. Michigan Avenue
Galesburg, MI 49053
E-mail: ensata@aol.com
Web site: www.ensata.com
Telephone: 616-665-7500
Fax: 616-665-7500
Japanese irises

Enviromental Concern
P.O. Box P
201 Boundry Lane
St. Michaels, MD 21663
E-mail: order@wetland.org
Web site: www.wetland.org
Telephone: 410-745-9620
Fax: 410-745-3517
Wetland native plants

Ericaceae
P.O. Box 293
Deep River, CT 06417-0293
Telephone: 860-526-5100
Ericaceous plants

Ernst Conservation Seeds
9006 Mercer Pike
Meadville, PA 16335-9299
E-mail: ernstsales@ernstseed.com
Web site: www.ernstseed.com
Telephone: 814-336-2404
Fax: 814-336-5191
Native seeds

229

COLLECTOR'S GUIDE

Fairweather Gardens
P.O. Box 330
Greenwich, NJ 08323
Web site: www.fairweathergardens.com
Telephone: 856-451-6261
Fax: 856-451-0303
Collector's trees, shrubs, and fancy perennials

Fancy Fronds
P.O. Box 1090
Gold Bar, WA 98251-1090
E-mail: judith@fancyfronds.com
Web site: www.fancyfronds.com
Telephone: 360-793-1472
Fax: 360-793-4243
Huge list of ferns

Fantastic Plants
5865 Steeplechase Drive
Bartlett, TN 38134-5509
E-mail: fanplant@aol.com
Web site: www.fantasticplants.com
Telephone: 901-438-1912
Fax: 901-372-6818
Unusual shrubs, trees, dwarf conifers, and Japanese maples

Fedco
P.O. Box 520
Waterville, ME 04903-0520
Web site: www.fedcoseeds.com
Telephone: 207-873-7333
Fax: 207-872-8317
Seeds, trees, shrubs, fruits, and perennials

Ferry-Morse Seeds
P.O. Box 488
Fulton, KY 42041-0488
E-mail: onlineorders@ferry-morse.com
Web site: www.ferry-morse.com
Telephone: 800-283-3400
Seeds

Fiddley Frond's Nursery
P.O. Box 252
7 Maine Street
Norridgewock, ME 04957
E-mail: cmetcalf@wworx.net
Telephone: 207-634-4918
Fax: 207-634-4918
Ferns and species lilies

Fieldstone Gardens
55 Quaker Lane
Vassalboro, ME 04989-3816
Web site: www.fieldstonegardens.com
Telephone: 207-923-3836
Fax: 201-923-3836
Perennials

Flickingers Nursery
P.O. Box 245
Sagamore, PA 16250
Telephone: 800-368-7381
Fax: 724-783-6528
Tree seedlings

The Flowery Branch Seed Company
P.O. Box 1330
Flowery Branch, GA 30542
E-mail: seedsman@hotmail.com
Telephone: 770-536-8380
Medicinal herbs

Foliage Gardens
2003 128th Avenue S.E.
Bellevue, WA 98005
E-mail: foliageg@juno.com
Web site: www.foliagegardens.com
Telephone: 425-747-2998
Ferns

Forestfarm
990 Tetherow Road
Williams, OR 97544-9599
E-mail: plants@forestfarm.com
Web site: www.forestfarm.com
Telephone: 541-846-7269
Fax: 541-846-6963
Huge list of trees, shrubs, vines, and perennials

Fox Hill Nursery
347 Lunt Road
Freport, ME 04032
E-mail: info@lilacs.com
Web site: www.lilacs.com
Telephone: 207-729-1511
Fax: 207-729-1511
Lilacs

The Fragrant Path
P.O. Box 328
Fort Calhoun, NE 68023
Fragrant annuals, perennials, trees, shrubs, and heirloom plants

Franklin Hill Garden Seeds
2430 Rochester Road
Sewickley, PA 15143-8667
E-mail: info@franklinhillseeds.com
Web site: www.franklinhillseeds.com
Telephone: 412-367-6202
Fax: 412-367-6202
Seeds

Garden in the Woods
180 Hemenway Road
Framingham, MA 01701-2699
E-mail: newfs@newfs.org
Web site: www.newfs.org
Telephone: 508-877-7630
Fax: 508-877-3658
Native plant seeds

Gardens North
5984 Third Line Road North
North Gower, ON K0A 2T0
Canada
E-mail: seed@gardensnorth.com
Web site: www.gardensnorth.com
Telephone: 613-489-0065
Fax: 613-489-1208
Hardy perennial seeds

Garden Vision
63 Williamsville Road
Hubbardston, MA 01452-4808
E-mail: darellpro@earthlink.net
Web site: www.home.earthlink.net/~darrellpro
Telephone: 978-928-4808
Fax: 978-928-4808
Epimediums and shade perennials

Geraniaceae
122 Hilcrest Avenue
Kentfiled, CA 94904
E-mail: geraniac@pacbell.net
Web site: www.geraniaceae.com
Telephone: 415-461-4168
Fax: 415-461-7209
Hardy geraniums and related genera

Girard Nurseries
P.O. Box 428
Geneva, OH 44041
E-mail: girardnurseries@suite224.net
Web site: www.girardnurseries.com
Telephone: 440-446-2881
Fax: 440-466-3999
Rhododendrons and evergreens

Glasshouse Works
P.O. Box 97
Church Street
Stewart, OH 45778-0097
E-mail: plants@glasshouseworks.com
Web site: www.glasshouseworks.com
Telephone: 740-662-2142
Fax: 740-662-2120
Tropical and subtropical plants, and succulents

Goodwin Creek Gardens
P.O. Box 83
Williams, OR 97544
E-mail: info@goodwincreekgardens.com
Web site: www.goodwincreekgardens.com
Telephone: 800-846-7359
Fax: 541-846-7357
Herbs, fragrant plants, and native species

Gossler Farms Nursery
1200 Weaver Road
Springfield, OR 97478-9691
Web site: www.gosslerfarms.com
Telephone: 541-746-3922
Fax: 541-744-7924
Unusual woody plants and hellebores

Russell Graham, Purveyor of Plants
4030 Eagle Crest Road N.W.
Salem, OR 97304
E-mail: grahams@open.org
Telephone: 503-362-1135
Collector's perennials, woodland wildflowers, lilies, and ferns

Great Basin Natives
P.O. Box 114
310 S. Main
Holden, UT 84636
E-mail: gbn@greatbasinnatives.com
Web site: www.greatbasinnatives.com
Telephone: 435-795-2303
Native trees, shrubs, perennials, and grasses

Greer Gardens
1280 Goodpasture Island Road
Eugene, OR 97401-1794
E-mail: orders@greergardens.com
Web site: www.greergardens.com
Telephone: 800-548-0111
Fax: 541-686-0910
Rhododenrons, spectacular woody plants, and hellebores

Grigsby Cactus Gardens
2354 Bella Vista Drive
Vista, CA 92084-7836
Telephone: 760 727-1323
Fax: 760-727-1578
Cacti and succulents

H & H Botanicals
P.O. Box 291
Bancroft, MI 48414
E-mail: orders@handhbotanicals.com
Telephone: 989-413-0257
Fax: 989-288-2514
Alpines and unusual herbaceous perennials

Harris Seeds
P.O. Box 24966
355 Paul Road
Rochester, NY 14624-0966
Web site: www.harrisseeds.com
Telephone: 800-514-4441
Fax: 877-892-9197
Seeds

Heaths & Heathers
502 E. Haskell Hill Road
Shelton, WA 98584-8429
E-mail:
handh@heathsandheathers.com
Web site: www.heathsandheathers.com
Telephone: 800-294-5318
Fax: 800-294-3284
Calluna, Erica, and other Ericaceae

Hedera Etc.
P.O. Box 461
Lindonville, PA 19353
E-mail: hedera@worldnet.att.net
Telephone: 610-970-9175
Ivies of all kinds

Heirloom Gardens
13889 Dupree Worthey Road
Harvest, AL 35749
E-mail: heriloomgardens@home.com
Web site: www.heirloomnursery.com
Telephone: 256-233-4422
Organically grown seeds of perennials, herbs, and others

Heirloom Roses
24062 N.E. Riverside Drive
St. Paul, OR 97137
E-mail: info@heirloomroses.com
Web site: www.heirloomroses.com
Telephone: 503-538-1576
Fax: 503-538-5902
Antique roses

Heirloom Seed Project
2451 Kissel Hill Road
Lancaster, PA 17601-4899
Telephone: 717-569-0401
Fax: 717-560-2147
Seeds of heirloom vegetables and ornamentals

Heirloom Seeds
P.O. Box 245
West Elizabeth, PA 15088-0245
E-mail: mail@heirloomseeds.com
Web site: www.heirloomseeds.com
Telephone: 412-384-0852
Fax: 412-384-0852
Seeds of heirloom varieties and strains

Heronswood Nursery
7530 N.E. 288th Street
Kingston, WA 98346-9502
E-mail: heronswood@silverlink.net
Web site: www.heronswood.com
Telephone: 360-297-4172
Fax: 360-297-8321
Rare and unusual collector's perennials and some woodies

Heritage Rose Gardens
40350 Wilderness Road
Branscomb, CA 95417
Telephone: 707-964-3748
Historical roses

High Altitude Gardens
4150 B Black Oak Drive
Hailey, ID 83333-8447
E-mail: orders@seedstrust.com
Web site: www.highaltitudegardens.com
Telephone: 208-788-4363
Fax: 208-788-3452
Seeds of alpines and Rocky Mountain natives

High Country Gardens
2902 Rufina Street
Sante Fe, NM 87505-2929
E-mail:
plants@highcountrygardens.com
Web site: www.highcountrygardens.com
Telephone: 800-925-9387
Fax: 800-925-0097
Drought-resistant perennials, collections, natives, grasses, and hardy cacti

J. L. Hudson, Seedsman
P.O. Box 337
Star Route 2
La Honda, CA 94020
E-mail: inquiry@jlhudsonseeds.net
Web site: www.jlhudsonseeds.net
Seeds of hard-to-find plants

Ion Exchange
1878 Old Mission Drive
Harpers Ferry, IA 52146-7533
E-mail: sales@ionxchange.com
Web site: www.ionxchange.com
Telephone: 800-291-2143
Fax: 563-535-7362
Native prairie seeds and plants

J & J Tranzplant Aquatic Nursery
P.O. Box 227
Wild Rose, WI 54984-0227
E-mail: jmalchow@tranzplant.com
Web site: www.tranzplant.com
Telephone: 800-622-5055
Fax: 715-256-0039
Water and bog plants and supplies

Johnny's Selected Seeds
955 Benton Avenue
Winslow, ME 04901-2601
E-mail: info@johnnyseeds.com
Web site: www.johnnyseeds.com
Telephone: 800-879-2258
Fax: 800-437-4290
Quality vegetable seeds

Joy Creek Nursery
20300 N.W. Watson Road
Scappoose, OR 97056
E-mail: catalogue@joycreek.com
Web site: www.joycreek.com
Telephone: 503-543-7474
Fax: 503-543-6933
Perennials, grasses, vines, and shrubs

J. W. Jung Seed Co.
335 S. High Street
Randolph, WI 53957
E-mail: info@jungseed.com
Web site: www.jungseed.com
Telephone: 800-297-3123
General seeds and plants

Klehm's Song Sparrow
13101 E. Rye Road
Avalon, WI 53505
E-mail: info@songsparrow.com
Web site: www.songsparrow.com
Telephone: 800-553-3715
Fax: 608-883-2257
Collector's perennials, peonies, and new woody plants

Laporte Avenue Nursery
1950 Laporte Avenue
Frort Collins, CO 80521
Alpine and rock garden plants

Lilypons Water Gardens
P.O. Box 10
6800 Lilypons Road
Buckeystown, MD 21717-0010
E-mail: info@lilypons.com
Web site: www.lilypons.com
Telephone: 800-999-5459
Fax: 800-879-5459
Water plants

Little Acre Farm
223 Victory Road
Howell, NJ 07731
Web site: www.littleacrefarm.com
Telephone: 732-938-6300
Fax: 732-938-6340
Bamboos and topiaries

Logee's Greenhouses
141 North Street
Danielson, CT 06239
Web site: www.logees.com/store
Telephone: 888-330-8038
Fax: 888-774-9932
Tropical plants, tender perennials, and vines

Louisiana Nursery
5853 Highway 182
Opelousas, LA 70570
Web site: www.durionursery.com
Telephone: 337-948-3696
Fax: 337-942-6404
Magnolias and hard-to-find shrubs

Maryland Aquatic Nurseries
3427 N. Furnace Road
Jarrettsville, MD 21084
E-mail: info@marylandaquatic.com
Web site: www.marylandaquatic.com
Telephone: 410-557-7615
Fax: 410-692-2837
Water lilies, tropical and hardy shallow-water plants and supplies

Matsu-Momiji Nursery
7520 Troy Stone Drive
Fuquay Varina, NC 27526
Web site: www.matsumomiji.com
Telephone: 919-552-2592
Japanese maples

McClure & Zimmerman
P.O. Box 368
108 W. Winnebago Street
Friesland, WI 53935-0368
E-mail: info@mzbulb.com
Web site: www.mzbulb.com
Telephone: 800-883-6998
Fax: 800-374-6120
Dutch bulbs

Merry Gardens
122 Mechanic Street
Camden, ME 04843
Telephone: 207-236-9064
Fax: 207-763-4168
Greenhouse plants

Miller Nurseries
5060 W. Lake Road
Canandaigua, NY 14424-8904
E-mail: info@millernurseries.com
Web site: www.millernurseries.com
Telephone: 800-836-9630
Fax: 716-396-2154
Fruiting plants

Miniature Plant Kingdom
4125 Harrison Grade Road
Sebastopol, CA 95472
E-mail: info@miniplantkingdom.com
Web site: www.miniplantkingdom.com
Telephone: 707-874-2233
Fax: 707-874-3242
Dwarf plants

Missouri Wildflowers Nursery
9814 Pleasant Hill Road
Jefferson City, MO 65109
E-mail: mowldflrs@sockets.net
Web site: www.mowildflowers.net
Telephone: 573-496-3492
Fax: 573-496-3003
Native perennials, annuals, grasses, trees, shrubs, and vines

Moon Mountain Wildflowers
P.O. Box 725
Carpinteria, CA 93014-0725
Telephone: 805-684-2565
Wildflower seeds

Mountain Crest Gardens
P.O. Box 724
Etna, CA 96027
E-mail: info@mc-garden-gifts.com
Web site:
www.mountaincrestgardens.com
Telephone: 877-656-4035
Fax: 530-467-5733
Rock garden plants and hardy succulents

Mountain Maples
P.O. Box 1329
54561 Registered Guest Road
Laytonville, CA 95454-1329
E-mail: mtmaples@mcn.org
Web site: www.mountainmaples.com
Telephone: 888-707-6522
Fax: 707-984-7433
Japanese maples

Mountain Mist Ornamentals
45525 S.E. Marmot Road
Sandy, OR 97055
E-mail: evattrk@worldnet.att.net
Telephone: 503-668-4637
Fax: 503-668-4637
Japanese and Siberian irises, and hostas

Munchkin Nursery & Garden
323 Woodside Drive N.W.
Depauw, IN 47115-9039
E-mail:
genebush@munchkinnursery.com
Web site: www.munchkinnursery.com
Telephone: 812-633-4858
Fax: 812-633-4858
Woodland wildflowers and shade perennials

Musser Forests
1880 Route 119 Highway North
Indiana, PA 15701
E-mail: info@musserforests.com
Web site: www.musserforests.com
Telephone: 800-643-8319
Fax: 724-465-9893
Liners for trees and shrubs, and young plants in bulk

Native American Seed
127 N. 16th Street
Junction, TX 76849
E-mail: info@seedsource.com
Web site: www.seedsource.com
Telephone: 800-728-4043
Fax: 800-728-3943
Native plant seeds

Native Gardens
5737 Fisher Lane
Greenback, TN 37742
E-mail: meredith@native-gardens.com
Web site: www.native-gardens.com
Telephone: 423-856-0220
Native plants

Native Seeds/SEARCH
526 N. 4th Avenue
Tucson, AZ 85705-8450
E-mail: info@nativeseeds.org
Web site: www.nativeseeds.org
Telephone: 520-622-5561
Fax: 520-662-5591
Traditional Native American crop seeds

Naylor Creek Nursery
2610 W. Valley Road
Chimacum, WA 98325
E-mail: naylorck@olypen.com
Web site: www.naylorcreek.com
Telephone: 360-732-4983
Fax: 360-732-7171
Hostas and collector's shade perennials

New England Bamboo Company
5 Granite Street
Rockport, MA 01966
E-mail: info@newengbamboo.com
Web site: www.newengbamboo.com
Telephone: 978-546-3581
Fax: 978-546-1075
Bamboos

New England Wildflower Society
180 Hemenway Road
Framingham, MA 01701
Web site: www.newfs.org/seeds04
Telephone: 508-877-7630
Fax: 508-877-3658
Native plant seeds and fern spores

New Peony Farm
P.O. Box 18235
St. Paul, MN 55118
E-mail: kent@newpeonyfarm.com
Web site: www.newpeonyfarm.com
Telephone: 651-457-8994
Peonies

Niche Gardens
1111 Dawson Road
Chapel Hill, NC 27516
E-mail: orders@nichegardens.com
Web site: www.nichegardens.com
Telephone: 919-967-0078
Fax: 919-967-4026
Native perennials, annuals, grasses, trees, shrubs, and native azaleas

Nicholls Gardens
4724 Angus Drive
Gainesville, VA 20155
E-mail: nichollsgardens@juno.com
Web site: www.nichollsgardens.com
Telephone: 703-754-9623
Fax: 703-754-9623
Irises, natives, and hybrids

Nichols Garden Nursery
1190 N. Pacific Highway
Albany, OR 97321-4580
E-mail: customersupport@
nicholsgardennursery.com
Web site:
www.nicholsgardennursery.com
Telephone: 800-422-3985
Fax: 800-231-5306
Herbs, vegetables, and seeds

Northwest Native Seed
17595 Vierra Canyon Road 172
Prunedale, CA 93907
E-mail: oreonana@juno.com
Seeds for wildflowers from western and mountain states

Oddysey Bulbs
8984 Meadow Lane
Berrien Springs, MI 49103
E-mail: mail@odysseybulbs.com
Web site: www.odysseybulbs.com
Telephone: 269-471-4642
Fax: 269-471-4642
Hardy and tender unusual bulbs

Oikos Tree Crops
P.O. Box 19425
Kalamazoo, MI 49019-0425
Web site: www.oikostreecrops.com
Telephone: 269-624-6233
Fax: 269-624-4019
Fruiting plants, nut trees, and magnolias

Old House Gardens
536 Third Street
Ann Arbor, MI 48103-4957
E-mail: charlie@oldhousegardens.com
Web site: www.oldhousegardens.com
Telephone: 734-995-1486
Fax: 734-995-1687
Heirloom bulbs

One Green World
28696 S. Cramer Road
Molalla, OR 97038-8576
E-mail: info@onegreenworld.com
Web site: www.onegreenworld.com
Telephone: 877-353-4028
Fax: 800-418-9983
Unique fruits and exotic ornamentals

Oregon Exotics Rare Fruit Nursery
1065 Messinger Road
Grants Pass, OR 97527
Web site: www.exoticfruit.com
Telephone: 541-846-7578
Fax: 541-846-9488
Unusual fruiting plants

Park Seed Co.
1 Parkton Avenue
Greenwood, SC 29647
E-mail: info@parkseed.com
Web site: www.parkseed.com
Telephone: 800-845-3369
Fax: 800-275-9941
Wide variety of seeds and plants

Peaceful Valley Farm Supply
P.O. Box 2209
Grass Valley, CA 95945
E-mail: contact@groworganic.com
Web site: www.groworganic.com
Telephone: 888-784-1722
Fax: 530-272-4794
Organic seeds, cover crops, natural pest and weed controls, and tools

Perennial Pleasures Nursery
P.O. Box 147
East Hardwick, VT 05836
E-mail: annex@perennial.com
Web site: www.perennialpleasures.net
Telephone: 802-472-5104
Fax: 802-472-3737
Heirloom annuals, perennials, and herbs

Perry's Water Gardens
136 Leatherman Gap Road
Franklin, NC 28734
E-mail: perrywat@dnet.net
Web site: www.tcfb.com/perwatg
Telephone: 828-524-3264
Fax: 828-369-2050
Water plants

Piccadilly Farm
1971 Whippoorwill Road
Bishop, GA 30621
Telephone: 706-769-6516
Hellebores, shade perennials, conifers, and woody plants

Pickering Nurseries
670 Kingston Road
Pickering. ON L1V 1A6
Canada
E-mail: roses@pickeringnurseries.com
Web site: www.pickeringnurseries.com
Telephone: 905-839-2111
Fax: 905-839-4807
Roses

Pine Ridge Gardens
832 Sycamore Road
London, AR 72847
E-mail: office@pineridgegardens.com
Web site: www.pineridgegardens.com
Telephone: 501-293-4359
Fax: 501-293-4659
Native woody and herbaceous plants

Pinelands Nursery
323 Island Road
Columbus, NJ 08022
E-mail: sales@pinelandnursery.com
Web site: www.pinelandsnursery.com
Telephone: 800-667-2729
Fax: 609-298-8939
Native plants and erosion controls

Pinetree Garden Seeds
P.O. Box 300
New Gloucester, ME 04260
E-mail: pinetree@superseeds.com
Web site: www.superseeds.com
Telephone: 207-926-3400
Fax: 888-527-3337
Seeds

Plant Delights Nursery
9241 Sauls Road
Raleigh, NC 27603
E-mail: office@ plantdelights.com
Web site: www.plantdelights.com
Telephone: 919-772-4794
Fax: 919-662-0370
*Hostas, aroids, ferns, grasses, woody and
herbaceous perennials, vines, groundcovers, bulbs,
and tubers*

Plant Pics' Perennials
P.O. Box 3224
Duluth, MN 55803
E-mail: cromso@charter.net
Telephone: 218-724-5988
Fax: 218-724-6164
Hostas and other shade perennials

Plantasia Cactus Gardens
867 Filer Avenue West
Twin Falls, ID 83301
Telephone: 208-734-7959
Cacti

Plants of the Southwest
3095 Agua Fria Road
Santa Fe, NM 87507
E-mail:
contact@plantsofthesouthwest.com
Web site:
www.plantsofthesouthwest.com
Telephone: 800-788-7333
Fax: 505-438-8800
Desert and dryland seeds and plants

Plants of the Wild
P.O. Box 866
Willard Field
Tekoa, WA 99033
E-mail: kathy@plantsofthewild.com
Web site: www.plantsofthewild.com
Telephone: 509-284-2848
Fax: 509-284-6464
Native plants

Pleasant Run Nursery
P.O. Box 247
Allentown, NJ 08501
Telephone: 609-259-8585
Fax: 609-259-6044
*Perennials, annuals, grasses, vines, trees,
and shrubs*

Prairie Moon Nursery
31837 Bur Oak Lane
Winona, MN 55987-9515
E-mail: info@prairiemoon.com
Web site: www.prairiemoon.com
Telephone: 507-452-1362
Fax: 507-454-5238
Native prairie and meadow seeds

Prairie Nursery
P.O. Box 306
Westfield, WI 53964
E-mail:
customerservice@prairienursery.com
Web site: www.prairienursery.com
Telephone: 800-476-9453
Fax: 608-296-2741
*Grasses, forbs, and flowering perennials of
the prairie*

Prairie Ridge Nursery
9738 Overland Road
Mt. Horeb, WI 53572-2832
E-mail: crmeco@chorus.net
Web site: www.prairieridgenursery.com
Telephone: 608-437-5245
Fax: 608-437-8982
*Native perennial and biennial forbs and grasses,
and seeds*

√ The Primrose Path
921 Scottdale-Dawson Road
Scottdale, PA 15683
E-mail: primrose@a1usa.net
Web site: www.theprimrosepath.com
Telephone: 724-887-6756
Fax: 724-887-3077
Heuchera, Tiarella, Asarum, Carex,
ferns, natives, and woodland plants

Puget Sound Kiwi Co.
1220 N.E. 90th Street
Seattle, WA 98115
Telephone: 206-523-6403
Fax: 206-523-6403
Kiwi and figs

Raintree Northwoods
391 Butts Road
Morton, WA 98356
E-mail: info@raintreenursery.com
Web site: www.raintreenursery.com
Telephone: 360-496-6400
Fax: 888-770-8358
Fruit trees, berries, and woody plants

Rarefind Nursery
957 Patterson Road
Jackson, NJ 08527
E-mail: info@rarefindnursery.com
Web site: www.rarefindnursery.com
Telephone: 732-833-0613
Fax: 732-833-1965
Rhododendrons and shrubs

Redwood City Seed Co.
P.O. Box 361
Redwood City, CA 94064
Web site: www.ecoseeds.com
Telephone: 650-325-7333
Fax: 650-325-4056
Western wildflower seeds

Richter's
357 Highway 47
Goodwood, ON L0C 1A0
Canada
E-mail: orderdesk@richters.com
Web site: www.richters.com
Telephone: 905-640-6677
Fax: 905-640-6641
Herbs and seeds

Riverdale Iris Gardens
4652 Culver Avenue N.W.
Buffalo, MN 55313
Telephone: 320-963-6810
Irises

Robinett Bulb Farm
P.O. Box 1306
Sebastopol, CA 95473-1306
Unusual bulbs and California native bulbs

Robyn's Nest Nursery
14324 206th Street S.E.
Snohomish, WA 98296
E-mail: karen@robynsnestnursery.com
Web site: www.robynsnestnursery.com
Telephone: 425-486-6919
Hostas and collector's perennials

Rock Spray Nursery
P.O. Box 693
Truro, MA 02666
E-mail: marketing@rockspray.com
Web site: www.rockspray.com
Telephone: 508-349-6769
Fax: 508-349-2732
Heathers and heaths

Rocky Mountain Rare Plants
1706 Deerpath Road
Franktown, CO 80116-9462
E-mail: staff@rmrp.com
Web site: www.rmrp.com
Fax: 775-201-2911
Alpine seeds from around the world

Roots & Rhizomes
P.O. Box A
Randolph, WI 53956-0118
E-mail: info@rootsrhizomes.com
Web site: www.rootsrhizomes.com
Telephone: 800-374-5035
Hostas, daylilies, irises, and others

The Roseraie at Granite Ridge
P.O. Box R
670 Bremen Road
Waldoboro, ME 04572-0919
Telephone: 207-832-6330
Fax: 800-933-4508
Roses

Roslyn Nursery
211 Burrs Lane
Dix Hills, NY 11746
E-mail: roslyn@roslynnursery.com
Web site: www.roslynnursery.com
Telephone: 631-643-9347
Fax: 631-427-0894
Collector's plants, rhododendrons, shrubs, trees, and perennials

Sandy Mush Herb Nursery
316 Surrett Cove Road
Leicester, NC 28748-5517
Telephone: 828-683-2014
Fax: 828-683-2014
Herbs

Savory's Gardens
5300 Whiting Avenue
Edina, MN 55439-1249
E-mail: savory@savorysgardens.com
Web site: www.savorysgardens.com
Telephone: 952-941-8755
Fax: 952-941-3750
Hostas

John Scheepers
23 Tulip Drive
Bantam, CT 06750-1631
E-mail:
customerservice@johnscheepers.com
Web site: www.johnscheepers.com
Telephone: 860-567-0838
Fax: 860-567-5323
Dutch bulbs

S. Scherer & Sons
104 Waterside Road
Northport, NY 11768
E-mail: lilyfishpond@aol.com
Web site: www.waterlilyfarm.com
Telephone: 631-261-7432
Fax: 631-261-9325
Water plants and supplies

Schipper & Co.
P.O. Box 7584
Greenwich, CT 06836
E-mail: info@colorblends.com
Web site: www.colorblends.com
Telephone: 888-847-8637
Fax: 203-862-8909
Bulbs

F. West Schumacher Co.
36 Spring Hill Road
Sandwich, MA 02563-1023
E-mail: treeseed@capecod.net
Web site: www.treeshrubseeds.com
Telephone: 508-888-0659
Seeds of trees and shrubs

Seed Savers Exchange
3076 N. Winn Road
Decorah, IA 52101
E-mail: tara@seedsavers.org
Web site: www.seedsavers.org
Telephone: 563-382-5990
Fax: 563-382-5872
Heirloom seeds

Seeds of Change
621 Old Santa Fe Trail #10
Santa Fe, NM 87506-5700
E-mail: gardener@seedsofchange.com
Web site: www.seedsofchange.com
Telephone: 888-762-7333
Organic seeds and seedlings, herbs, vegetables, and flowers

Seeds of Distinction
P.O. Box 86, Station A
Toronto, ON M9C 4V2
Canada
E-mail: seeds@seedsofdistinction.com
Web site: www.seedsofdistinction.com
Telephone: 416-255-3060
Fax: 888-327-9193
Hard-to-find seeds

Seeds West Garden Seeds
317 14th Street N.W.
Albuquerque, NM 87104
E-mail: seeds@nmia.com
Web site:
www.seedswestgardenseeds.com
Telephone: 505-843-9713
Western wildflowers, herbs, and chili peppers

Select Plus International Lilac Nursery
1510 Pine
Mascouche, QC J7L 2M4
Canada
E-mail: lilacs@axess.com
Web site: www.spi.8m.com
Telephone: 450-477-3797
Fax: 450-477-3797
Large selections of lilacs

Select Seeds Antique Flowers
180 Stickney Hill Road
Union, CT 06076-4617
E-mail: info@selectseeds.com
Web site: www.selectseeds.com
Telephone: 860-684-0395
Fax: 800-653-3304
Heirloom flowers, seeds, and plants

Seneca Hill Perennials
3712 County Route 57
Oswego, NY 13126
E-mail: hornig@usadatanet.net
Web site: www.senecahill.com
Telephone: 315-342-5915
Fax: 315-342-5573
Arisaema, Arum, hardy South African plants, and species peonies

Shady Oaks Nursery
P.O. Box 708
1601 5th Street S.E.
Waseca, MN 56093-3122
E-mail: shadyoaks@shadyoaks.com
Web site: www.shadyoaks.com
Telephone: 507-835-5033
Fax: 507-835-8772
Hostas, Asarum, and other shade perennials

Shepherd Iris Garden
3342 W. Orangewood
Phoenix, AZ 85051-7453
E-mail: bobbieshep@aol.com
Telephone: 602-841-1231
Fax: 602-841-1231
Bearded irises

R. H. Shumway's
P.O. Box 1
Graniteville, SC 29829-0010
E-mail: info@rhshumway.com
Web site: www.rhshumway.com
Telephone: 803-663-9771
Fax: 888-437-2733
General seeds and plants

Shooting Star Nursery
444 Bates Road
Frankfort, KY 40601-9446
E-mail: shootingstarnursery@msn.com
Web site: www.shootingstarnursery.com
Telephone: 502-223-1679
Fax: 502-227-5700
Native wildflowers of the Eastern U.S.

Singing Springs Nursery
8802 Wilkerson Road
Cedar Grove, NC 27231
E-mail:
plants@singingspringsnusery.com
Web site:
www.singingspringsnursery.com
Telephone: 919-732-9403
Fax: 919-732-6336
Tender plants and hardy perennials

Siskiyou Rare Plant Nursery
2825 Cummings Road
Medford, OR 97501
E-mail: customerservice@srpn.net
Web site: www.srpn.net
Telephone: 541-772-6846
Fax: 541-772-4917
Hardy plants, alpine and rock garden plants, and conifers

Slocum Water Gardens
1101 Cypress Gardens Boulevard
Winter Haven, FL 33884-1932
Web site:
www.slocumwatergardens.com
Telephone: 863-293-7151
Fax: 800-322-1896
Water plants

Southern Exposure
35 Minor Street
Beaumont, TX 77702-2414
Telephone: 409-835-0644
Fax: 409-835-0644
Seeds of southern native plants

Southern Exposure Seed Exchange
P.O. Box 460
Mineral, VA 23117
Web site: www.southernexposure.com
Telephone: 540-894-9480
Untreated heirloom vegetable, herb, and flower seeds

Springdale Water Gardens
P.O. Box 546
340 Old Quarry Lane
Greenville, VA 24440-0546
E-mail:
info@springdalewatergardens.com
Web site:
www.springdalewatergardens.com
Telephone: 800-420-5459
Fax: 540-337-0738
Water lilies, bog plants, and supplies

Squaw Mountain Gardens
P.O. Box 946
Estacada, OR 97023
E-mail:
sales@squawmountaingardens.com
Web site:
www.squawmountaingardens.com
Telephone: 503-637-3585
Fax: 503-637-3580
Hardy succulents

St. Lawrence Nurseries
325 State Highway 345
Potsdam, NY 13676
E-mail: trees@sln.potsdam.ny.us
Web site: www.sln.potsdam.ny.us
Telephone: 315-265-6739
Northern-climate fruit and nut trees

Stark Bro's
P.O. Box 1800
Louisiana, MO 63353-1800
E-mail: info@starkbros.com
Web site: www.starkbros.com
Telephone: 800-325-4180
Fax: 573-754-8880
Fruit and ornamental trees

Sticks & Stones Farm
197 Huntingtown Road
Newtown, CT 06470
E-mail:
moss@sticksandstonesfarm.com
Web site:
www.sticksandstonesfarm.com
Mosses

Stockton Iris Gardens
P.O. Box 55195
Stockton, CA 95205
Telephone: 209-462-8106
Irises

Stokes Seeds
P.O. Box 548
Buffalo, NY 14240
E-mail: stokes@stokeseeds.com
Web site: www.stokeseeds.com
Telephone: 800-263-7233
Fax: 888-834-3334
Vegetable and cut-flower seeds

Stokes Tropicals
4806 E. Old Spanish Trail
Jeanerette, LA 70544-6018
E-mail: info@stokestropicals.com
Web site: www.stokestropicals.com
Telephone: 800-624-9706
Fax: 337-365-6991
Tropicals and subtropicals

Strong's Alpine Succulents
P.O. Box 50115
Parks, AZ 86018
Telephone: 928-635-1127
Alpine succulents

Sunlight Gardens
174 Golden Lane
Andersonville, TN 37705
E-mail: info@sunlightgardens.com
Web site: www.sunlightgardens.com
Telephone: 800-272-7396
Fax: 865-494-7086
Wildflowers, vines, ferns, and shrubs

Sunny Boy Gardens
3314 Earlysville Road
Earlysville, VA 22936
Web site: www.sunnyboygardens.com
Telephone: 804-974-7350
Herbs, accesories, and gifts

Swan Island Dahlias
P.O. Box 700 Department 1
Canby, OR 97013
E-mail: info@swanislanddahlias.com
Web site: www.swanislanddahlias.com
Telephone: 800-410-6540
Fax: 503-266-8768
Dahlias

Sylva Native Nursery & Seed Co.
1683 Sieling Farm Road
New Freedom, PA 17349
E-mail: plants@sylvanative.com
Web site: www.sylvanative.com
Telephone: 717-227-0486
Fax: 717-227-0484
Native trees, shrubs, and herbaceous plants

The Temple Nursery
P.O. Box 591
Trumansburg, NY 14886
Rare Galanthus *bulbs*

Territorial Seed Co.
P.O. Box 158
Cottage Grove, OR 97424-0061
E-mail: tertrl@territorial-seed.com
Web site: www.territorial-seed.com
Telephone: 541-942-9547
Fax: 888-657-3131
Organic vegetable, fruit, and herb seeds and plants, and tools and supplies

The Thomas Jefferson Center for
Historic Plants
P.O. Box 316
Charlottesville, VA 22902
E-mail: twinleaf@monticello.org
Web site: www.monticello.org
Telephone: 434-984-9821
Historic American garden seeds and plants

Thompson & Morgan
P.O. Box 1308
Jackson, NJ 08527-0308
E-mail: tminc@thompson-morgan.com
Web site: www.thompson-morgan.com
Telephone: 800-274-7333
Fax: 888-466-4769
Hard-to-find seeds of ornamental and green-house plants

Toadshade Wildflower Farm
53 Everittstown Road
Frenchtown, NJ 08825
E-mail: toadshad@toadshade.com
Web site: www.toadshade.com
Telephone: 908-996-7500
Fax: 908-996-7500
Native perennial wildflower plants

Tradewinds Bamboo Nursery
28446 Hunter Creek Loop
Gold Beach, OR 97444
E-mail: gib@bamboodirect.com
Web site: www.bamboodirect.com
Telephone: 541-247-0835
Fax: 541-247-0835
Bamboo plants, barriers, and tools

Tranquil Lake Nursery
45 River Street
Rehoboth, MA 02769-1395
E-mail: dchogan@sprynet.com
Web site: www.tranquil-lake.com
Telephone: 508-252-4002
Fax: 508-252-4740
Daylilies and Siberian and Japanese irises

Trees of Antiquity
20 Wellsona Road
Paso Robles, CA 93446
E-mail: neil@treesofantiquity.com
Web site: www.treesofantiquity.com
Telephone: 805-467-2509
Fax: 805-467-9909
Antique apple varieties

Trennoll Nursery
P.O. Box 125
3 W. Page Avenue
Trenton, OH 45067-0125
Telephone: 513-988-6121
Fax: 513-424-003
Rock garden plants, perennials, and wildflowers

William Tricker
7125 Tanglewood Drive
Independence, OH 44131
Web site: www.tricker.com
Telephone: 800-524-3492
Fax: 216-524-6688
Water lilies and pond supplies

Trillium Gardens
P.O. Box 803
Pleasant Hill, OR 97455
Telephone: 541-937-3073
Fax: 541-937-2261
Northwest natives

Tripple Brook Farm
37 Middle Road
Southampton, MA 01073
E-mail: info@tripplebrookfarm.com
Web site: www.tripplebrookfarm.com
Telephone: 413-527-4626
Fax: 413-527-9853
Eastern native and underused exotic plants

Underwood Gardens
1414 Zimmerman Road
Woodstock, IL 60098
E-mail: info@underwoodgardens.com
Web site: www.underwoodgardens.com
Telephone: 815-338-6279
Fax: 888-382-7041
Heirloom seeds

Underwood Shade Nursery
P.O. Box 1386
North Attleboro, MA 02763-0386
E-mail:
info@underwoodshadenursery.com
Web site:
www.underwoodshadenursery.com
Telephone: 508-222-2164
Fax: 508-222-5152
Shade perennials, ferns, and grasses

Van Bourgondien Bros.
P.O. Box 1000
Babylon, NY 11702
E-mail: blooms@dutchbulbs.com
Web site: www.dutchbulbs.com
Telephone: 800-622-9959
Fax: 800-327-4268
Dutch bulbs and perennials

Van Engelen
23 Tulip Drive
Bantam, CT 06750-5323
E-mail:
customerservice@vanengelen.com
Web site: www.vanengelen.com
Telephone: 860-567-8734
Fax: 860-567-5323
Dutch bulbs and perennials

Van Ness Water Gardens
2460 N. Euclid Avenue
Upland, CA 91784-1199
E-mail: vnwg@vnwg.com
Web site: www.vnwg.com
Telephone: 800-205-2425
Fax: 909-949-7217
Water and bog plants, and supplies

Variegated Foilage Nursery
245 Westford Road
Eastford, CT 06242
Web site: www.variegatedfoliage.com
Telephone: 860-974-3951
Fax: 860-974-3951
Variegated plants

Vesey's Seeds
P.O. Box 9000
Charlottetown, PEI C1A 8K6
Canada
E-mail: veseys@veseys.com
Web site: www.veseys.com
Telephone: 800-363-7333
Fax: 800-686-0329
General seeds and plants

Andre Viette Farm and Nursery
P.O. Box 1109
Fishersville, VA 22939
E-mail: viette@viette.com
Web site:
www.inthegardenradio.com/nursery
Telephone: 540-943-2315
Fancy perennials and daylilies

Vintage Gardens
2833 Old Gravenstein Highway South
Sebastapol, CA 95472
E-mail: gita@vintagegardens.com
Web site: www.vintagegardens.com
Telephone: 707-829-2035
Fax: 707-829-9516
Antique roses

Wade and Gatton Nursery
1288 Gatton Rocks Road
Bellville, Ohio 44813
Telephone: 419-883-3191
Huge selection of hostas

Waterford Gardens
74 E. Allendale Road
Saddle River, NJ 07458
E-mail: splash@waterfordgardens.com
Web site: www.waterfordgardens.com
Telephone: 201-327-0721
Fax: 201-327-0684
Water and bog plants and supplies

Water Mill Gardens
1280 Enterprise-Osteen Road
Enterprise, FL 32725-9401
E-mail: dtrimm56@aol.com
Web site: www.trimmerdaylily.com
Telephone: 386-574-2789
Daylilies

Wayside Gardens
1 Garden Lane
Hodges, SC 29695-0001
Web site: www.waysidegardens.com
Telephone: 800-213-0379
Fax: 800-817-1124
Fancy shrubs, trees, and perennials

We-Du Nurseries
2055 Polly Spout Road
Marion, NC 28752-7348
E-mail: info@we-du.com
Web site: www.we-du.com
Telephone: 828-738-8300
Woodland wildflowers

Weird Dude's Plant Zoo
1164 Frog Pond Road
Staunton, VA 24401
E-mail:
info@ weirddudesplantzoo.com
Web site:
www.weirddudesplantzoo.com
Telephone: 540-886-6364
Fax: 540-885-8223
Self-described "Awesome Plants"

Well-Sweep Herb Farm
205 Mount Bethel Road
Port Murray, NJ 07865
E-mail: herbs@goes.com
Web site: www.wellsweep.com
Telephone: 908-852-5390
Fax: 908-8521649
Herbs and flowering perennials

White Flower Farm
P.O. Box 50
Route 63
Litchfield, CT 06759-0050
E-mail: custserv@whiteflowerfarm.com
Web site: www.whiteflowerfarm.com
Telephone: 800-503-9624
Fax: 860-482-0532
*Annuals, bulbs, perennials, shrubs, vines, and
kitchen-garden plants*

Whitney Gardens & Nursery
P.O. Box 170
Brinnon, WA 98320-0080
E-mail: info@whitneygardens.com
Web site: www.whitneygardens.com
Telephone: 800-952-2404
*Kalmia, Rhododendron, azaleas, and
magnolias*

Gilbert H. Wild and Son
3044 State Highway 37
Sarcoxie, MO 64862-0338
Web site: www.gilberthwild.com
Telephone: 888-449-4537
Fax: 888-548-6831
Daylilies and peonies

Wild Earth Native Plant Nursery
49 Mead Avenue
Freehold, NJ 07728
E-mail:
wildearthnpn@compuserve.com
Telephone: 732-308-9777
Fax: 732-308-9777
Native plants

Wildginger Woodlands
P.O. Box 1091
Webster, NY 14580-7791
E-mail: bcmmin@frontiernet.net
Native plants and seeds

Wilkerson Mill Gardens
9595 Wilkerson Mill Road
Plametto, GA 30268
Webstie: www.hydrangea.com
Telephone: 770-463-2400
Fax: 770-463-9717
Hydrangeas and other flowering shrubs

Woodlanders
1128 Colleton Avenue
Aiken, SC 29801
E-mail: woodland@scbn.net
Web site: www.woodlanders.net
Telephone: 803-648-7522
Fax: 803-648-7522
*Woody plants, yuccas, herbaceous perennials,
grasses, ferns, subtropical plants, bulbs, and
tubers*

Woodside Nursery
327 Beebe Run Road
Bridgeton, NJ 08302
Web site: www.woodsidenursery.com
Telephone: 856-451-2162
Fax: 856-541-2280
Daylilies

Wrightman Alpines
RR#3
1503 Napperton Drive
Kerwood, ON N0M 2B0
Canada
E-mail: info@wrightmanalpines.com
Web site: www.wrightmanalpines.com
Telephone: 519-247-3751
Fax: 519-247-3751
Rock garden and alpine plants

Guy Wrinkle Exotic Plants
11610 Addison Street
North Hollywood, CA 91601
E-mail: guywrinkle@rareexotics.com
Web site: www.rareexotics.com
Telephone: 310-670-8637
Fax: 310-670-1427
Tropical plants

Yerba Buena Nursery
19500 Skyline Boulevard
Woodside, CA 94062
Web site: www.yerbabuenanursery.com
Telephone: 650-851-1668
Fax: 650-851-5565
California native plants

Yucca Do Nursery
P.O. Box 907
Hempstead, TX 77445
E-mail: info@yuccado.com
Web site: www.yuccado.com
Telephone: 979-826-4580
Fax: 979-826-4571
Collector's plants and hardy palms

PLANT SOCIETIES

If you are a bona fide plant nut, then you might be interested in meeting similarly deranged individuals. Object: Maybe if there are enough of us, then everyone else will seem a little less crazy. Obsession loves company.

Chances are collectors who share your passion are eager to welcome you to their plant society. The benefits of joining include learning more about a species, genus, or family and sharing the wisdom of others on growing these plants well. Through meetings, conventions, publications letters, and even E-mail, you will meet like-minded enthusiasts who can share their secrets, tips, and tricks on breaking the code of how to germinate a difficult seed or the best soil mix with which to grow a certain plant. Best of all, there is the chance to obtain new species, cultivars, or hybrids—from seeds or cuttings or even from a pollen exchange with members.

The societies' publications are frequently scholarly journals, but just as often, they are lighthearted ramblings of one plant freak to another; for example, the American Fern Society publishes *Fiddlehead Forum*; the Tuber Society prints *Tater Talk*.

Some of the larger societies are often more general in scope. The Hardy Plant Society is a British institution, but there are North American chapters: the Mid-Atlantic Group and the Hardy Plant Society of Oregon and of New England. The Northwest's organization has a yearly three-day symposium. Hardy Plant Society types are fervent devotees. One year, their meeting might have as its theme *Ranunculaceae*, the buttercup family including clematis, columbine, hellebore, and delphinium. The group would bring in experts from all over the United States, Canada, Britain, and around the world for sold-out lectures and demonstrations.

Besides the comradeship, society meetings nearly always present opportunities to buy plants. At the Northwest's Hardy Plant Society meeting in Seattle in the summer of 1994, for example, some of the best local nurseries (wholesale and retail) sold their most esoteric bounty under a tent set up in the parking lot.

The Perennial Plant Association, an American organization, consists mostly of professionals. Its wonderful quarterly magazine presents articles on the latest growing methods as well as the top plants of the moment. The organization also chooses and promotes a plant of the year and sponsors yearly summer trips to different parts of the United States; reportedly, these trips are not only the most illuminating—with visits to gardens and growers that would be impossible to see any other way—but also are wild—busloads of plantaholics adding a pot or two to the crowded coach at every stop.

The serious and venerable American Rhododendron Society offers research grants and scholarships as well as seed, plant, and pollen exchanges. Joining one of their many chapters is a great way to meet some of the best amateur and professional growers in the country (and world).

Perhaps the most impressive society of all is the esteemed North American Rock Garden Society. One of the best ways to find unusual plants is through their seed exchanges. Rock gardeners are known for their devotion to alpines, but they accept a wide variety of plants into their dominion, including many woodland plants as well as conifers and others. Plants are worshiped at Rock Garden Society meetings. The peak achievement a member can accomplish is to get a very rare plant to flower from seed. Photographic proof is usually required. Nevertheless, the only thing that society members want more than a new plant is a new member, so you will be graciously welcomed. Although this may be the most highbrow of all the organizations, its quarterly magazine is informative and easy to understand.

Additional societies with seed exchanges are the Alpine Garden Society in Vancouver, British Columbia; the American Primrose Society in Oregon; and, in the United Kingdom, the Alpine Garden Society, the Hardy Plant Society, the Cyclamen Society, and the Scottish Rock Garden Club. See below for addresses for the groups mentioned here and for many other societies. The address listed is the home of a board member, and these officers may change from year to year. Try the Web sites below, or search the Web for the society names.

Alpine Garden Society
The Secretary
AGS Centre, Avonbank
Pershore, Worcestershire WR10 3JP
England
Web site: www.alpinegardensociety.org
Telephone: +44 (0) 1386 554 790
Fax: +44 (0) 1386 554 801

American Bamboo Society
Membership Secretary
750 Krumkill Road
Albany, NY 12203-5957
Web site: www.americanbamboo.org
Telephone: 518-458-7617
Fax: 518-458-7625

American Bonsai Society
Executive Secretary
420 Eberle Drive
Toledo, OH 43615
Web site: www.absbonsai.org

American Clematis Society
Edith Malek
P.O. Box 17085
Irvine, CA 92623-7085
Web site: www.clematis.org

American Conifer Society
P.O. Box 3422
Crofton, MD 21114-0422
Web site: www.conifersociety.org
Telephone: 410-721-6611
Fax: 410-721-9636

The American Daffodil Society
4126 Winfield Road
Columbus, OH 43220-4606
Web site: www.daffodilusa.org

American Dahlia Society
Alan A. Fisher
ADS Membership
1 Rock Falls Court
Rockville, MD 20854
Web site: www.dahlia.org

American Dianthus Society
Rand B. Lee
President
P.O. Box 22232
Santa Fe, NM 87502-2282
Telephone: 505-438-7038

American Fern Society
Missouri Botanical Garden
P.O. Box. 299
St. Louis, MO 63166-0299
Web site: www.amerfernsoc.org

American Fuchsia Society
Judy Salome
6979 Clark Road
Paradise, CA 95969
Web site:
www.americanfuchsiasociety.org

American Hemerocallis Society
Pat Mercer
AHS Executive Secretary
Department WWW
P.O. Box 10
Dexter, GA 31019
Web site: www.daylilies.org

American Hepatica Association
Paul Held
195 North Avenue
Westport, CT 06880

American Hibiscus Society
4231 Shamrock Drive
Venice, FL 34293
Web site: www.americanhibiscus.org

American Horticultural Society
7931 E. Boulevard Drive
Alexandria, VA 22308-1300
Telephone: 800-777-7391
Web site: www.ahs.org

American Hosta Society
AHS Membership Secretary
8702 Pinnacle Rock Court
Lorton, VA 22079-3029
Web site: www.hosta.org

The American Hydrangea Society
P.O. Box 11645
Atlanta, GA 30355-1645
Web site:
www.americanhydrangeasociety.org

American Iris Society
Membership Secretary
P.O. Box 2968
Baltimore, MD 21229
Web site: www.irises.org

American Ivy Society
P.O. Box 2123
Naples, FL 34106-2123
Web site: www.ivy.org

American Orchid Society
16700 AOS Lane
Delray Beach, FL 33446-4351
Web site: www.orchidweb.org
Telephone: 561-404-2000

American Penstemon Society
Ann Bartlett
1569 S. Holland Court
Lakewood, CO 80232
Web site:
www.biosci.ohio-state.edu/~awolfe/
Penstemon/Penstemon.html

The American Peony Society
Claudia Schroer
713 White Oak Lane
Gladstone, MO 64116-4607
Web site:
www.americanpeonysociety.org
Telephone: 816-459-9386
Fax: 816-459-7430

American Primrose Society
Julia L. Haldorson
Treasurer
P.O. Box 210913
Auke Bay, AK 99821
Web site:
www.americanprimrosesoc.org

American Rhododendron Society
Executive Director
11 Pinecrest Drive
Fortuna, CA 95540
E-Mail: oars@arsoffice.org
Web site: www.rhododendron.org
Telephone: 707-725-3043

American Rose Society
P.O. Box 30000
Shreveport, LA 71130-0030
Telephone: 800-637-6534
Web site: www.ars.org

American Sakurasoh Association
Paul Held
195 North Avenue
Westport, CT 06880
E-mail: asa@sakurasoh.com
Web site: www.sakurasoh.com

The American Violet Society
AVS Membership Coordinator
Violet Hill Farm
356 Windsor Street
Randolph, ME 04346
E-mail:
violet@americanvioletsociety.org
Web site:
www.americanvioletsociety.org

Australian Plants Society
Michelle Wilson
P.O. Box 744
Blacktown, NSW
Australia 2148
E-mail: : office@austplants-nsw.org.au
Web site: www.austplants-nsw.org.au
Telephone: +61 (02) 9621 3437
Fax: +61 (02) 9676 7603

The Azalea Society of America
Bob Stelloh
ASA Treasurer
65 Sierra Drive
Hendersonville, NC 28735-7963
Web site: www.azaleas.org

Cactus & Succulent Society of America
Mindy Fusaro
P.O. Box 2615
Pahrump, NV 89041-2615
E-mail: cssa@wizard.com
Web site: www.cssainc.org
Telephone: 775-751-1320

The Canadian Wildflower Society
Business Secretary
Unit 12A, Box 228
4981 Highway #7 East
Markham, ON L3R 1N1
Canada
Telephone: 905-294-9075
Fax: 416-466-6428

The Cycad Society
Fairchild Tropical Garden
10901 Old Cutler Road
Miami, FL 33156

The Cyclamen Society
Dr. D. V. Bent
Little Pilgrims
2 Pilgrims Way East
Otford, Sevenoaks
Kent TN14 5QN
England
E-mail: membership@cyclamen.org
Web site:
www.cyclamen.org/indexCS.html
Telephone: +44 (0) 1959 522 322

The Daffodil Society UK
Mrs. J. Pearson
Hofflands
Bakers Green
Little Totham
Maloon, Essex CM9 8LT
England
Telephone: +44 (0) 1621 788 678

Geraniaceae Group
Membership Secretary
Peter Starling
22 Northfields
Girton
Cambridge CB3 0QG
England
E-mail: cranesbill_1999@yahoo.com
Web site:
www.geocities.com/RainForest/
Canopy/3139

The Hardy Fern Foundation
Membership
P.O. Box 166
Medina, WA 98036-0166
E-mail: hff@hardyferns.org
Web site: www.hardyferns.org

Hardy Plant Society
Mrs. Pam Adams
Little Orchard, Great Comberton
Pershore, Worcestershire WR10 3DP
England
E-mail: admin@hardy-plant.org.uk
Web site: www.hardy-plant.org.uk
Telephone: +44 (0) 1386 710 317
Fax: +44 (0) 1386 710 117

Hardy Plant Society——Mid-Atlantic
Group
Pat Horowitz
801 Concord Road
Glen Mills, PA 19342
E-mail: wilkin1380@aol.com
Web site: www.hardyplant.org
Telephone: 610-558-2857

The Hardy Plant Society of Oregon
1930 N.W. Lovejoy Street
Portland, OR 97209-1504
Web site: www.hardyplantsociety.org
Telephone: 503-224-5718

Heartland Peony Society
Jim Crist
15738 Horton Lane
Overland Park, KS 66223
Web site: www.peonies.org

The Herb Society of America
9019 Kirtland Chardon Road
Kirtland, OH 44094
Web site: www.herbsociety.org
Telephone: 440-256-0514

Heritage Roses Group
Northwest Area Coordinator
Helen Pressley
P.O. Box 7606
Olympia, WA 98507
E-mail: hpre461@aol.com
Web site:
thefragrantgarden.com/hrg.html

Holly Society of America
HSA Secretary
309 Buck Street
P.O. Box 803
Millville, NJ 08332-0803
Telephone: 856-825-4300
Web site: www.hollysocam.org

International Aroid Society
Membership
P.O. Box 43-1853
South Miami, FL 33143-1853
E-mail: tricia_frank@hotmail.com
Web site: www.aroid.org

International Asclepiad Society
L. B. Deiderfield
2 Keymer Court
Burgess Hill, West Sussex RH15 0AA
England

International Black Plants Society
Karen Platt
35 Longfield Road
Crookes
Sheffield S10 1QW
England
E-mail: k@karenplatt.co.uk
Web site:
www.karenplatt.co.uk/ibps.htm

International Bulb Society
P.O. Box 336
Sanger, CA 93657-0336
Web site: www.bulbsociety.com

International Carnivorous Plant
Society
P.O. Box 330
3310 E. Yorba Linda Boulevard
Fullerton, CA 92831-1709
Web site: www.carnivorousplants.org

International Geranium Society
IGS Membership
Dept. WWW
P.O. Box 92734
Pasadena, CA 91109-2734
Web site:
www.geocities.com/RainForest/2822

International Lilac Society
3 Paradise Court
Cohoes, NY 12047-1422
Web site: lilacs.freeservers.com

The International Palm Society
P.O. Box 1897
Lawrence, KS 66044-8897
E-mail: palms@allenpress.com
Web site: www.palms.org

The Magnolia Society
Roberta Hagen
6616 81st Street
Cabin John, MD 20818
Web site: www.magnoliasociety.org

National Auricula & Primula Society
Peter Ward
6 Lawson Close
Saltford, Somerset BS18 3LB
England

National Chrysanthemum Society
Galen Goss, Secretary
10107 Homar Pond Drive
Fairfax Station, VA 22039-1650
Web site: www.mums.org

National Gardening Association
1100 Dorset Street
South Burlington, VT 05403
Web site: www.garden.org
Telephone: 802-863-5251

North American Dianthus Society
Rand B. Lee
P.O. Box 22232
Santa Fe, NM 87502-2232
E-mail: randbear@nets.com

North American Gladiolus Council
NAGC Membership Secretary
1387 Augusta Road
Belgrade, ME 04917-3732
Web site:
www.empirestategladiolus.com/nagc

North American Lily Society
Dr. Robert Gilman, NALS Executive
Secretary
P.O. Box 272
Owatonna, MN 55060
Web site: www.lilies.org

North American Rock Garden Society
P.O. Box 67
Milwood, NY 10546
Web site: www.nargs.org

Northwest Perennial Alliance
Membership Secretary
c/o Susan McKinney
13322 120th Avenue N.E.
Kirkland, WA 98024
E-mail: membership@
northwestperennialalliance.org
Web site:
www.northwestperennialalliance.org
Telephone: 425-814-1481

Passiflora Society International
c/o Butterfly World
3600 W. Sample Road
Coconut Creek, FL 33073
E-mail: info@passiflora.org
Web site: www.passiflora.org
Telephone: 954-977-4434
Fax: 954-977-4501

Rhododendron Society of Canada
R. S. Dickhout
5200 Timothy Crescent
Niagara Falls, ON L2E 5G3
Canada
Web site: www.rhodoniagara.org
Telephone: 905-356-3432
Fax: 905-375-0018

The Royal Horticultural Society
Membership Secretary
P.O. Box 313
80 Vincent Square
London SW1P 2PE
England
Web site: www.rhs.org.uk
Telephone: +44 (0) 1718 344 333
Fax: +44 (0) 1716 306 060

Rose Hybridizers Association
Mr. Larry D. Peterson
21 S. Wheaton Road
Horseheads, NY 14845
Web site: www.rosehybridizers.org

Sedum Society
Sue Haffner
3015 Timmy
Clovis, CA 93612-4849
E-mail: sue_haffner@csufresno.edu
Web site: www.cactus-mall.com/sedum

Seed Savers Exchange
3076 N. Winn Road
Decorah, Iowa 52101
Web site: www.seedsavers.org
Telephone: 563-382-5990

Species Iris Group of North America
Rodney Barton
3 Wolters Street
Hickory Creek, TX 75065-3214
Web site: www.signa.org

The Succulent Society of South Africa
Private Bag X10, 0028 Hatfield
Pretoria, South Africa
E-mail: sssa@succulents.net
Web site: www.succulents.net/society
Telephone: +27 (12) 993 3588
Fax: +27 (12) 993 3588

SUGGESTED READING

American Association of Botanical Gardens and Arboreta. *Directory of Gardens in North America.* Wilmington, Delaware: American Association of Botanical Gardens and Arboreta, 1998.

Armitage, Allan M. *Herbaceous Perennial Plants.* Second Edition. Champaign, Illinois: Stipes Publishing Company, 1998.

Avent, Tony. *So You Want to Start a Nursery.* Portland, Oregon: Timber Press, 2003.

Bailey, Liberty Hyde. *Hortus Third: A Concise Dictionary of Plants Cultivated in the United States and Canada.* Revised and expanded by the staff of the Liberty Hyde Bailey Hortorium, Cornell University. New York: Macmillan, 1976.

Berkeley, Edmund, and Dorothy Smith Berkeley. *The Life and Travels of John Bartram: From Lake Ontario to the River St. John.* Tallahassee: Florida State University, 1982.

Bir, Richard E. *Growing and Propagating Showy Native Woody Plants.* Chapel Hill and London: University of North Carolina Press, 1992.

Bown, Deni. *Aroids.* Second Edition. Portland, Oregon: Timber Press, 2000.

Clebsch, Betsy. *The New Book of Salvias: Sages for Every Garden.* Portland, Oregon: Timber Press, 2003.

Darke, Rick. *The American Woodland Garden.* Portland, Oregon: Timber Press, 2002.

Dirr, Michael A. *Manual of Woody Landscape Plants.* Fifth Edition. Champaign, Illinois: Stipes Publishing Company, 1998.

Druse, Ken. *Ken Druse: The Passion for Gardening: Inspiration for a Lifetime.* New York: Clarkson Potter, 2003.

————. *Making More Plants: The Science, Art, and Joy of Propagation.* New York: Clarkson Potter, 2000.

————. *The Natural Habitat Garden.* Portland, Oregon: Timber Press, 2004.

————. *The Natural Shade Garden.* New York: Clarkson Potter, 1992.

Eddison, Sydney. *The Self-Taught Gardener.* New York: Penguin, 1998.

Glattstein, Judy. *Consider the Leaf.* Portland, Oregon: Timber Press, 2003.

Graf, Alfred Byrd. *Tropica.* Fifth Edition. Rutherford, New Jersey: Roehrs Company, 2003.

Hillier Nurseries. *The Hillier Manual of Trees and Shrubs.* Pocket Edition. Wiltshire, Great Britain: David and Charles, 2002.

Hinkley, Daniel. *The Explorer's Garden.* Portland, Oregon: Timber Press, 1999.

Phillips, Roger, and Martin Rix. *The Botanical Garden.* Toronto: Firefly Books, 2002.

Springer, Lauren. *The Undaunted Garden.* Golden, Colorado: Fulcrum Publishing, 1994.

Thompson, Peter. *Creative Propagation.* Second Edition. Portland, Oregon: Timber Press, in press.

INDEX

The entries below include the page numbers where topics are found in the text. Numbers in **bold** type indicate photographs. References to the USDA minimum temperature zones (defined below) are noted in *italics* at the end of each plant entry. Hardiness for some cultivars are given as a general guideline in parentheses with the genus entry—*Hemerocallis* spp. (*Z4*), for example.

The abbreviation (a) tells that a plant is most often grown as an annual. An accompanying zone number tells: (1) if the number is lower than 9 (as in the case of California poppy), the seed is hardy and the plant may return after winter as a self-sown new plant; or, (2) if higher than 9 (as in the case of *Coleus*), that the plant is a tender perennial killed by frost. Plants in the latter category may be lifted and stored for the winter in a frost-free place—even the window garden if in active growth, and replanted in the spring.

Quite a few of the plants in this book are new to horticulture and have been grown only in limited locations. Their zone information has been estimated from anecdotal evidence. Some plants have not been tested and have no zone reference number. If you want to try a plant that you suspect might not be hardy enough for your area, consider that there are micro-climates around your property, such as near the foundation of the house, that can make it possible for the plant to survive. Remember the experiences of the Colorado gardeners in this book who grow herbaceous plants that are not rated for their climate. A reliable snow cover and, even more, excellent drainage can lead to root survival of many herbaceous plants.

The primary sources for checking plant names were *The Plant Finder*, devised and compiled by Chris Philip, edited by Tony Lord, published by Headman for The Royal Horticultural Society, England; and *Hortus Third*, by the staff of the L. H. Bailey Hortorium, Cornell University, published by Macmillan. In some cases collectors have provided the information.

USDA Hardiness Zone numbers and the average minimum temperature (Fahrenheit) on which they are based:

Z1: below −50°; *Z2*: −50° to −40°; *Z3*: −40° to −30°; *Z4*: −30° to −20°; *Z5*: −20° to −10°; *Z6*: −10° to 0°; *Z7*: 0° to 10°; *Z8*: 10° to 20°; *Z9*: 20° to 30°; *Z10*: 30° to 40°; *Z11*: 40° plus